CHRIST ABOVE ALL

THE BOOK OF COLOSSIANS

DAVID JEREMIAH

with Dr. David Jeremiah

© 2022 Turning Point for God
P.O. Box 3838
San Diego, CA 92163
All Rights Reserved

www.DavidJeremiah.org

Edited by Robert J. Morgan

Printed in the United States of America.

Contents

Christ Above All

WHEN DID YOU LAST PICK UP A PEN, GRAB A PIECE OF stationary, and compose an honest-to-goodness letter to someone? Letter writing is a lost art, but it shouldn't be. Your meaningful handwritten notes will probably land in a keepsake drawer and add to a treasured memory, while all our texts and emails can be deleted with the press of a button.

Frank Blake liked to write letters, and he was a gifted correspondent. He learned from the best: George H. W. Bush. Bush was also a dedicated letter writer, and when he served as Vice President, Blake served as his deputy counsel.

"Vice President Bush started every day by typing notes to people," Blake said. "You knew they were typed by him because some of the letters were off line and there could be misspellings. I saw the power of taking the time to write a nice word to someone."

When Blake became CEO of The Home Depot in 2007, he set up a process for writing notes of encouragement to those in the company. Each store would send specific examples of excellent customer service to the district managers, the district managers would send their favorite picks to the regional managers, and the regional managers would send their top picks straight to Blake. On Sunday of each week, Blake would spend several hours writing notes by hand to thank his team for the amazing things they did each week. In all, he estimates he wrote more than 25,000 notes during his seven-year career at Home Depot!

"It was a great way for me to end the week," he says. "In an age of email and texts, there is something personal and special about a handwritten note."[1]

Colossians is one of history's most famous handwritten letters—one of thirteen by the apostle Paul. It's one of the smallest books in the Bible, made up of only 95 verses. It can easily be read in about ten minutes—but the understanding and application of its message is no short-term project.

There's a story behind this letter, which I'd like to share with you.

The city of Colossae was located in the Lycus Valley in what is now modern Turkey. In its heyday, the city was densely populated and wealthy, but by Paul's time it was dwarfed by the larger cities of Hierapolis and Laodicea. (Some years later, a devastating earthquake struck Colossae, and it was never rebuilt.)

How did the Colossian church begin? As far as we know, Paul never visited Colossae, and he was not the founder of the church there. That honor goes to a native Colossian—an unsung hero named Epaphras (Colossians 1:7). Most scholars believe Epaphras was converted as the result of Paul's three-year ministry in the metropolis of Ephesus, over one hundred miles away (Acts 19; 20:17-38).

Ephesus was a teeming port city, and this became the headquarters for much of Paul's ministry during his third missionary journey. As the apostle preached and taught in Ephesus, his converts took the Gospel back to their own towns and villages. In this way much of Asia Minor was evangelized. Acts 19:10 says, "All who dwelt in Asia heard the word of the Lord Jesus, both Jews and Greeks."

Apparently, Epaphras was one of those converts. He was gloriously saved while listening to Paul in Ephesus, and he took the Gospel back to his hometown, planting a church among his family and friends in Colossae.

A decade later, Paul was under house arrest in Rome, and Epaphras tracked him down. In the process, Epaphras may himself have been arrested (Philemon 23). I suspect Epaphras had ventured to Rome because his Colossian church was under attack. Some popular but destructive teachings had wormed their way into the fellowship, weakening the church and its core beliefs.

Epaphras may have believed he lacked the theological firepower or apostolic authority to refute the false teachers. So he came pleading for Paul's help, and Paul responded to Epaphras' request with this letter we call Colossians.

Since both he and Epaphras were now under house arrest, Paul commissioned Tychicus and Onesimus to deliver the letter to the Colossians (Colossians 4:7-9).

What false teaching does the book of Colossians confront? We can only put together the clues in the book itself. We have no external description of what has become known as the "Colossian Heresy."

What we glean from the book of Colossians is a picture of a complex heresy—a deceptive combination of many things: Eastern philosophy, Jewish legalism, pagan astrology, mysticism, asceticism, and warped Christianity. Most scholars believe it was a form of Gnosticism. The word *gnostic* comes from a Greek word meaning "to know." The Gnostics were people who claimed they knew hidden truths and had special knowledge of secret information. They were the spiritually elite "woke" religionists who had all the answers and looked with disdain on all those who were not yet enlightened.

According to Dr. A. T. Robertson, Gnostics believed that "God is good and hence could not touch matter. Therefore they believed that the world was created by intermediate agencies called aeons (emanations from God) who came in between God and matter. On accepting Christianity they at once had trouble with the Person of Christ. Where would He come in their system? They solved the problem by making Him one of the subordinate aeons."[2]

If that sounds confusing to you, join the club. Scholars have been trying to explain Gnosticism for a long time, but its very purpose was to confuse believers. Paul took on the Colossian heresy in this little letter to help true believers there and elsewhere deal with the false doctrine that was all around them. Because of this, Colossians has striking relevance today when our core Christian beliefs are under attack, both in and out of the Church.

In Colossians, the Lord led the apostle Paul to paint one of the most vivid portraits of Jesus Christ in all of Scripture in order to help us believers understand that Christ is above all and superior to any belief system promoted by any false voices.

Today there are thousands of ideas about the Person of Jesus Christ, but only one Book has it right—the Bible. In Colossians, we see our Lord in His infinite glory before the world came into being. We see Him divesting Himself of the trappings of glory to plunge into the mire of history. We see His matchless form as He gives His life for humanity. We feel the earthquake of His resurrection, watch His ascension to the throne, and see Him seated at the right hand of Majesty, with angels, powers, and dominions subject to Him.

The devil thought he was confusing the Colossians; instead, he was creating the occasion for God's great apostle to compose a timeless letter clarifying the doctrine of—and glorifying the Person of—our supreme Christ!

How often Satan goes too far! How gracious is God to thwart his attacks and send us a blessing instead!

As you read and study Colossians, you'll come to better know who Jesus is theologically. In other words, the truth about Him—the whole truth and nothing but the truth—will thrill you. Our minds need solid doctrine.

We need solid doctrine so we'll have a solid relationship with Christ, built on personal reverence for Him and friendship with

Him. The Jesus of Colossians is alive, interactive, victorious, and supreme. He's enthroned as Supreme Commander in heaven, and His return is imminent.

Unlike Frank Blake, not everyone can work with a president or vice president as a mentor. Most of us cannot imagine what it would be like to walk into the White House and call it our workplace, but it's a low privilege compared to loving, knowing, serving, and worshiping the Lord Jesus Christ who is high and exalted over all people.

In Paul's handcrafted letter, written from house arrest in Rome to a confused church in Asia Minor, you'll find glory in every verse, Jesus in every line, and a blessing in every chapter.

Let's study it together.

CHAPTER 1

Singing the Praises of the Unsung

COLOSSIANS 1:1-8

CHARLES PLUMB, A FARM BOY FROM KANSAS, BECAME a United States jet fighter pilot who completed 74 combat missions in Vietnam before being shot down on his last mission. Plumb ejected and parachuted into enemy hands, where he spent six years in a Vietnamese prison.

After his release, Plumb and his wife were at a restaurant when a man approached them. "You're Plumb! You flew jet fighters in Vietnam from the aircraft carrier *Kitty Hawk*. You were shot down!"

Plumb didn't know the fellow and wondered how he had gotten that information. The man explained, "I packed your parachute."

Then, pumping Plumb's hand, the man said, "I guess it worked!"

"It sure did. If your chute hadn't worked, I wouldn't be here today," said the pilot.[1]

Since his release, Charles Plumb has been a powerful motivational speaker, telling his story to hundreds of people. This incident often comes up. Charles Plumb has never gotten over his gratitude for the man who packed his parachute, and he often asks his audiences, "Who's packing your parachute?"[2]

In other words, who are the people behind the scenes in your life who care for you, help you, encourage you, and strengthen you, even if they often go unrecognized? And are you packing the parachute for someone else?

The Bible is filled with unsung heroes, and we meet several of them in the book of Colossians. As you read this short book, you'll come across names like Tychicus, Onesimus, Aristarchus, Mark, Justus, Luke, Nymphas, Archippus, and Epaphras. Except for Mark and Luke, few of the people in Colossians are household names, but they played a vital supporting role in the ministry of history's first great evangelist and missionary— Paul the apostle.

We want to be like them!

With that in mind, let's begin our study of Colossians by noticing how Paul opened the letter. In the first eight verses, he referred to three individuals and to one group of people.

The Author Was Paul the Apostle

He began, as he often did, with the words, "Paul, an apostle of Jesus Christ" (Colossians 1:1). Paul wrote Colossians near the end of his service for Christ. Nearly thirty years had passed since his Damascus Road experience, and now he was imprisoned in Rome during what we believe to be his first imprisonment, which we read about in Acts 28. During this period he wrote his Prison Epistles—Ephesians, Philippians, Colossians, and Philemon.

At this time, the false teachers who had invaded Colossae would challenge the credibility of anyone outside their cult, so Paul properly called attention to his rank and to his right to speak as a protagonist of true Christianity and against Gnostic heresy. The word "apostle" is related to the Greek word for "sent," and it implied Jesus Christ had sent Paul to evangelize the world.

John Phillips wrote:

Paul was an apostle, made a member of that unique and exclusive order by "the ordination of the nail-pierced hands." His particular calling was to be the apostle to the Gentiles. As such, he had a passion for people everywhere. The whole world was his parish, lost souls in all lands were his special charge, and the church of God was his dear love .... It was imperative that the Colossians understand that Paul was writing to them in his official capacity .... That they would be foolish to take his letter lightly.[3]

Paul didn't take on the role of apostleship by himself. The hand of Jesus was on him, compelling him by the Holy Spirit to preach the Gospel. Christ had sent him to do His work, and his reference to "the will of God" is a further reminder that his message and mission were from God and not from man.

You may not call yourself by the title "apostle," but something changes in our lives when we realize we, too, are sent by Jesus to spread His message wherever we go. It's exhilarating to view one's life as an ongoing series of nonstop opportunities to serve our supreme Savior. What an experience for even the humblest child of God!

The Associate Was Timothy the Brother

Verse 1 continues, "Paul, an apostle of Jesus Christ by the will of God, and Timothy our brother." If opposites attract, we can understand why Paul and Timothy were friends. Paul was strong, aggressive, and visionary. From all we can tell, Timothy was shy, timid, and frail. But the bond between them was undeniable. Paul even said there was no other friend with whom he was so like-minded as Timothy, giving him the title "my dearly beloved son" (2 Timothy 1:2, KJV). Speaking to the Philippians, he said of Timothy, "I have no one like-minded. . . . That as a son with his father he served with me in the gospel" (Philippians 2:20-22).

We have clues about Timothy from the Early Church historian Eusebius, who reported that after Paul's death, Timothy became the bishop or overseer of the churches in Ephesus. Timothy was probably about forty years old, and that became his center of ministry. According to one tradition, Timothy was present at the death of Mary, whose tomb is said to be near Ephesus. The same tradition suggests Timothy was martyred (stoned to death) in A.D. 97.[4]

Two men—as different from each other as they were indispensable to each other.

My mentor, Howard Hendricks, used to say we should all have at least two types of people in our lives: a Paul and a Timothy.

A *Paul* is an older man who is willing to mentor you, to build into your life. Not someone who's smarter or more gifted than you, but somebody who's been down the road. Somebody willing to share their strengths and weaknesses—everything he's learned in the laboratory of life. Somebody whose faith you'll want to imitate.

A *Timothy* is a younger man into whose life you are building. For a model, read 1 and 2 Timothy. Here was Paul, the quintessential mentor, building into the life of his protege—affirming, encouraging, teaching, correcting, directing, praying.[5]

Do you have these types of people in your life?

When author and speaker Jon Gordon was in high school, he tried to quit lacrosse during his freshman year. His coach, Tony Caiazza, wouldn't let him. Instead, he told John that he was going to play in college one day. He even said Jon would play in the Ivy League!

Jon didn't even know what the Ivy League was, but a few years later he ended up going to Cornell University to play for Coach Richie Moran, who also believed in him. The experience changed his life forever.

"The difference between success and failure is belief," Jon says. "And so often this belief is instilled in us by someone else . . . . You can be that person for the people you lead if you believe in them and see their potential rather than their limitations. It's amazing what people will accomplish when they know you believe in them!"[6]

Paul believed in Timothy enough to attach the young man's name along with his own at the top of this immortal letter. As one author put it:

> Paul was putting his name to a letter that would outlast all of the suns and stars of space. He was signing a "God-breathed" epistle, one of only twenty-one such letters ever to be written. Here was a writing destined to become part of the living Word of the living God, an instrument to bring light and life to millions of people for thousands of years, a document to outlast empires, and a letter that will be of absorbing interest to God's people in all the ages of eternities yet to be. And what does Paul do? He summons his young convert and colleague. He hands him his pen. He says, "Here you are, Timothy. Sign here. Now! Your name is linked with mine forever and wherever this letter will be read."[7]

This is a window into the heart of Paul, and it helps us to understand why God used him so greatly.

The Addressees Were the Faithful Brethren in Colossae

Verse 2 gives us the immediate recipients of this letter: "To the saints and faithful brethren in Christ who are in Colossae: Grace to you and peace from God our Father and the Lord Jesus Christ. We give thanks to the God and Father of our Lord Jesus Christ, praying always for you" (Colossians 1:2-3).

Epaphras had brought Paul a report about a threat to the church, but he had also brought lots of good news. From Epaphras, Paul knew much about the Colossian church and its people. He knew many of them were entrenched in their faithfulness to Christ.

When a man and woman marry, they promise to be faithful to one another, which means total commitment to an exclusive love. It's a terrible thing if doubts creep into the relationship. In the same way, the Bible exhorts us to be devoted exclusively to Jesus Christ.

Four times in Colossians, Paul uses the word "faithful" to describe those to whom he is writing. Here in Colossians 1:2, he addressed the entire church as "faithful brethren." In verse 7, he spoke of "Epaphras ... who is a faithful minister." Later he called Tychicus, "a beloved brother, faithful minister" (4:7); and Onesimus, "a faithful and beloved brother, who is one of you" (4:9).

Adrian Rogers wrote, "Faithfulness *does not* mean that we will be perfect. It *does not* mean that we won't struggle or that we won't make poor decisions. It *does* mean that we will continue to trust in God and *try* to follow His commandments even when life is difficult."[8]

The Designation of the Church

Paul also used the word "saints" to describe the church in Colossae: "To the saints and faithful brethren in Christ" (Colossians 1:2).

Some of the newer translations use the word *holy* to translate the word that's rendered "saint" in the New King James Version. The reason is because saint no longer conveys its biblical meaning in our culture. We think of saints as either dead heroes in church history or do-gooders who try to out-virtue everyone else.

One of the most beloved figures in British mystery is called *The Saint*, based on his initials—Simon Templar—and his crime-fighting, Robin Hood persona. But the man was always operating on the edge of the law, and now he's been relegated to black-and-white reruns.

One of our NFL teams is the New Orleans Saints.

So just what is a saint?

That word is God's way of describing His redeemed people!

"A 'saint' in the New Testament is not some person who has been canonized … immortalized in a stained glass window, and whose relics are worshiped and supposed to perform miracles. A saint is simply any sinner who is saved by grace."[9]

The New Testament doesn't use the word "saint" in reference to the *condition* of a person but to the *position* of the person. If you've accepted Jesus Christ as your Lord and Savior, you are, by God's definition, a saint. I am a saint—"Saint David."

Honestly, I wouldn't put that on my business card; people would misunderstand. But God attached that description to me the moment I confessed Jesus Christ as my Lord.

The same is true for you!

Our biblical status as saints is not based on any good works we have done, but on the righteousness of Jesus Christ. It's not a reputation we have to build; it's an identity we're able to display through the merits of Christ.

The Doxology of the Church

The apostle Paul goes on to speak a word of blessing over the Church in verse 2: "Grace to you and peace from God our Father and the Lord Jesus Christ."

This doxology is framed in a particular order. First grace and then peace. There can be no peace until there is grace.

There's no richer word in the New Testament than *grace*. It is the distinctive word of the work of Christ that sustains us from conversion all the way to heaven. Peace follows grace like a contrail follows a plane or a wake follows a motorboat.

Peace can be had in Christ, even in the midst of war. And if we had more of the grace of Christ, we would have more real peace in our hearts and lives. There's no deep peace without divine grace, and woe to a world that seeks the former without receiving the latter.

Do you feel you need more grace for the pressures of today? There's more available than you know!

Charles Spurgeon told of an evening when he was riding home after a long day's work. Feeling weary and depressed, he thought of 2 Corinthians 12:9, "My grace is sufficient for you."

He said, "I should think it is" and burst out laughing. He said that it seemed to make doubting God's grace absurd. It was as though some little fish, being very thirsty, was troubled about drinking the river dry, and the river said, "Drink away, little fish, my stream is sufficient for you." Or a man away up on a mountain saying to himself, "I fear I will exhaust all the oxygen in the atmosphere."[10]

The Description of the Church

Beginning with Colossians 1:3, Paul launches into an uplifting set of compliments and encouragements directed at the believers in Colossae. He begins this section saying, "We give thanks."

In Paul's original Greek, he begins his sentence in verse 3 and doesn't end it until verse 8—one long declaration of prayer and thanksgiving. Even though Paul's purpose in writing was to correct error, he began on a positive note, commending these believers for their Christlike qualities:

> As we take up Paul's letter, we immediately see that the apostle did not directly attack the Colossian problem, but rather began with an exuberant introduction that celebrated the Colossian church. This was typical of Paul, who characteristically praised churches before dealing with them pastorally. Paul's heartfelt commendation rose from the miracle that had taken place in Colossae: a poor, pagan people without God and without hope in this world had found Christ. Their lives had been changed, and some remarkable things had happened, which Paul will duly note.

His celebration was honest, and beautiful, and the celebration is ours as well—for we are the Church.[11]

Oh, if we could only learn this it would lift entire layers of heaviness from our hearts. Yes, your husband isn't perfect. Yes, you're burdened for your wife. Yes, your children are breaking your heart. Yes, your church is divided on some issue.

But before focusing all your attention on the problem, praise God for anything and everything you can find that's positive in the situation, like looking for sunbeams on a cloudy day. There's never a situation so dire or a tragedy so great as to exclude all basis for gratitude.

"Lord, even though this is bad, let me begin by thanking You for ...."

That is power praying!

He Celebrated Their Faith

Paul began by celebrating the faith of this little church. He wrote, "Since we heard of your faith in Christ Jesus" (Colossians 1:4). They did not just have faith; they had faith *in Jesus Christ*. When people say they are "people of faith," we have the right to ask them to tell us about the object of their faith. Faith in itself is worthless. The Colossians had faith in Jesus Christ.

One pastor asked, "Are you making the mistake of examining your faith rather than the Person upon which that faith should rest? If you were traveling a new public highway and approached a bridge whose strength you were not certain of, would you stop to examine your faith in that bridge or dismount and examine the structure itself? Common sense would tell you to examine the bridge, and then, when satisfied of its strength, you would cross over with confidence. So, look away to the promises that were made by God and trust Him."[12]

If you'll keep focused on Christ and His promises, your faith will rest secure.

He Celebrated Their Love

Paul also celebrated the love he saw among the Colossians, saying, "And of your love for all the saints" (Colossians 1:4). On the eve of His crucifixion, Jesus gave His disciples these instructions: "A new commandment I give to you, that you love one another; as I have loved you, that you also love one another" (John 13:34).

The apostle John was with Jesus that night, and he later became the last surviving apostle. His great topic was love. He featured love in his Gospel, and love dominated his first epistle. Listen to these verses:

- "We know that we have passed from death to life, because we love the brethren. He who does not love his brother abides in death" (1 John 3:14).

- "And this is His commandment: that we should believe on the name of His Son Jesus Christ and love one another, as He gave us commandment" (1 John 3:23).

Tradition says that as John got older, he reached the point where he preached of nothing other than love. I imagine that occasionally, some impatient member of the audience would interrupt him: "John, you've already preached that one. Tell us something new!"

"Very well," the beloved disciple would say with a smile. "A new commandment I give to you—that you love one another."

"When we have this love 'for all the saints,' there will be no more church politics, no more pampering of the rich at the expense of the poor, no more respect of people according to skin color."[13]

In his book *Hidden in Plain Sight: The Secret of More*, author and pastor Mark Buchanan tells the story of Tracy, one of the worship leaders at his church. One Sunday morning following a chaotic and messy week, Tracy "felt spent with nothing more to give."

When she crawled out of bed and walked into the living room that morning, she saw that the window was covered with writing from her eight-year-old daughter, Brenna. Brenna had taken a crayon and scribbled something across the window.

At first, Tracy was annoyed, thinking it was just one more mess to clean up. But then she saw what her daughter had written: *love, joy, peace, patience, kindnece, goodnece, faithfulnece, gentlnece and selfcantrol.*

Tracy stopped for a moment and realized that the message on her window was the reminder she needed. She could choose to face the day in the power of the Spirit! Then she noticed one more sentence at the edge of the window: Love one another. Only Brenna had written the second word differently: Love *won* another.

Pastor Buchanan said, "It's what Jesus has been trying to tell us all along. You were won that way. Now go and do likewise."[14]

He Celebrated Their Hope

But there's more! The apostle Paul also celebrated the hopefulness that filled the hearts of the Colossians. He wrote, "Because of the hope which is laid up for you in heaven, of which you heard before in the word of the truth of the gospel" (Colossians 1:5).

Someone said, "Faith rests on the past; love works in the present; hope presses toward the future."

Warren Wiersbe wrote: "Paul taught that hope is a motivating power for love and for faith .... I have noticed that the prospect of a future happiness has a way of making people love one another more. Have you watched children just before Christmas or a family vacation? The bright promise of heaven encourages our faith and expands our love. Then faith and love work together to make the present more enjoyable and the future more exciting."[15]

Now notice this: Not only is this hope being kept for us, but we ourselves are being protected by God's power so we can be certain to enjoy heaven one day. Listen to what Peter wrote in his first letter:

> Blessed be the God and Father of our Lord Jesus Christ, who according to His abundant mercy has begotten us again to a living hope through the resurrection of Jesus Christ from the dead, to an inheritance incorruptible and undefiled and that does not fade away, reserved in heaven for you, who are kept by the power of God through faith for salvation ready to be revealed in the last time (1 Peter 1:3-5).

Just before Clark Cothern's mom passed away she said, "After I'm gone, keep your eyes out for the gold." Clark and his sister chalked this admonition up to a little memory loss, but, just in case, they kept their eyes open. As the siblings sorted through their mom's things shortly after she went to heaven, they looked under drawers, behind cabinets—anywhere they thought she might have hidden some gold.

One day, Clark went to the bank to get the life insurance policy from his mom's safety deposit box. In a tiny room, all by himself, he opened the long narrow metal box. And under the life insurance policy was a brown paper lunch bag. He opened the crinkly paper sack, and there were two, three-inch long rolls of gold coins. He laughed out loud.

The gold was just as shiny as the day his mom had purchased it more than forty years ago. And it was a lot more valuable than the day it had been purchased. It had been kept safe as part of their inheritance.[16]

That's a little bit like the hope that is laid up in heaven for us. And that's something to celebrate!

Are you watching out for the gold?

We have a city gilded in gold and coming in glory! Why shouldn't we be brimming with hope?

He Celebrated Their Growth

Paul wasn't done. He went on in verse 6 to describe how the Gospel, which had come to them, "is bringing forth fruit, as it is also among you since the day you heard and knew the grace of God in truth" (Colossians 1:6).

The Colossians, though only a small church in a small city, were part of a great and growing work. Do you think any of the members of that church in the Lycus Valley could have imagined that two thousand years later we'd be studying their church and the small letter addressed to them?

As time passes, our work grows stronger—and it keeps on going after we're in heaven. Yes, Paul was under arrest and the Colossians were facing deceptive teachers, but God was growing them—and He was growing His Kingdom through them.

It's the very same for you!

Along the same lines, Paul was celebrating the growth of the Gospel around the world. Look at Colossians 1:6 again: "Which has come to you, as it has also in all the world, and is bringing forth fruit."

In all the world!

New Testament scholar David Garland wrote:

The gospel was bursting forth in small groups of Christians not only in such vital centers of the empire as Rome, Corinth, and Ephesus, but also in declining towns such as Colosse, in the hearts of slaveowners such as Philemon, and in runaway slaves such as Onesimus. The gospel is growing the way kudzu takes over in some parts of the American South. Originally imported as a groundcover, kudzu overruns everything. The difference is that the gospel is not some alien import or a noxious infestation but something deeply rooted in human need and in God's purposes for the whole creation.[17]

"Just as a tree without fruit and growth would no longer be a tree, so a gospel that bore no fruit would cease to be a gospel."[18]

That's good news! The power for change and growth doesn't come from us, but from the message we proclaim. That's why Paul could say in the book of Romans: "For I am not ashamed of the gospel of Christ, for it is the power of God to salvation for everyone who believes, for the Jew first and also for the Greek" (1:16).

This reminds me of the Bellavista prison in Medellin, Columbia. For many years it was one of the worst prisons in all of Latin America. "Bellavista's death toll ran as high as sixty a month as rival groups extended their warfare into the prison's maze of cardboard and scrap wood cubicles where inmates were quartered.

"In January 1990, inmates rioted after daily violence prompted prison guards to walk off the job. Local leaders called on the Colombian army to intervene. But days into the standoff, Oscar Osorio, a former Bellavista convict who became prison chaplain, gathered a handful of Christian volunteers associated with Chuck Colson's Prison Fellowship International. Singing hymns and carrying white flags, Osorio and his volunteers marched in procession through the prison gates, unsure if their lives would be spared.

"Osorio found the prison's public address system was still working, so he boldly called prisoners to repentance. Stunning prison authorities, the inmates laid down their weapons. The riot was over. But more than that, the killing stopped and the gospel swept through Bellavista like holy fire."[19]

In prisons, in refugee camps, in restricted nations, and all over the world, it's the Gospel that's making the difference. You are on the victorious side! You and I are part of the greatest redemptive movement in the history of earth. I think that's something for which to praise God!

The Assistant Was Epaphras the Servant

And now we come to this man, Epaphras. As I said earlier, he was the convert who took the Gospel back to Colossae and planted the church by sharing with his family and friends the truth that had changed his life.

Colossians 1:7-8 says, "As you also learned from Epaphras, our dear fellow servant, who is a faithful minister of Christ on your behalf, who also declared to us your love in the Spirit."

Later I'll show you another passage in Colossians about this man, emphasizing the power and fervor of his prayer life (Colossians 4:12).

It is one thing to minister at a moment of crisis, and all of us have had the opportunity to do that—to rise to the occasion of a great need. But it is something quite different to be ministering faithfully year after year and punctuating our service with our prayers. That's what Paul said about Epaphras. He was a minister who was faithful, whose protracted ministry was observable and worthy of mention.

Doesn't it make us long for more like him?

Doesn't it make us long to be like Christ?

Colossians for Today

With all that in mind, I want to end this chapter by focusing on three practical lessons from Colossians 1:1-8. As I've studied these verses, they have changed my own heart. Let me share a trio of takeaways with you.

Little Is Much if God Is in It

First, it's all right if we're not the biggest! In his classic commentary on the book of Colossians, J. B. Lightfoot claimed that "Colossae was the least important church to which any epistle of Paul was addressed."[20] It's likely the city would never have been mentioned in the New Testament had it not been for the church there. Here was a church of unknown people, in a small town, receiving an inspired letter from the great apostle Paul!

I don't see how the church in Colossae could have had more than thirty or forty people in it. The church meetings were held in the home of Philemon and his wife Apphia (Philemon 1:2), and the congregation itself had been started by a relatively unknown person: "You learned about the Good News from Epaphras" (Colossians 1:7, NLT).

Epaphras teaches us that God often uses unsung heroes to do His work. This man was an unknown man from a city that doesn't even exist today, yet he was instrumental in planting and establishing a healthy, thriving New Testament Church.

God doesn't need an apostle or pastor or full-time Christian worker to establish a ministry. All it takes is a person willing to tell others about the grace of God, a person ready to start loving others right where they are.

If we are willing to yield ourselves to God, there's no limit to what He will do through us. There's a Gospel song that dates back to 1924, written by Kittie L. Suffield. Though it's nearing a century mark, I still think it captures this truth:

> In the harvest field now ripened
> There's a work for all to do;
> Hark! The voice of God is calling
> To the harvest calling you.
>
> Little is much when God is in it,
> Labor not for wealth or fame;
> There's a crown and you can win it,
> If you go in Jesus' name.
>
> Does the place you're called to labor
> Seem too small and little known?
> It is great if God is in it,
> And He'll not forget His own.

Faithfulness Is Heaven's Badge of Honor

In applying this passage from Colossians to our lives, I've also got to circle back to the subject of faithfulness. Notice how many times faithfulness shows up in the story of this little church.

- "To the saints and faithful brethren in Christ who are in Colosse" (Colossians 1:2).

- "Epaphras, our dear fellow servant, who is a faithful minister of Christ on your behalf" (Colossians 1:7).

- "Tychicus, a beloved brother, faithful minister, and fellow servant in the Lord" (Colossians 4:7).

- "Onesimus, a faithful and beloved brother, who is one of you" (Colossians 4:9).

Entrepreneur Renee Zou wrote:

As I grow as a Christian ... I see that God usually works in us, not apart from our ordinary lives, but through them. He develops our Christ-likeness through the daily grace of inconspicuous opportunities.

Meanwhile, grandiose and dramatic notions of service now seem dangerously unrealistic. I realise that they romanticise the lives of God's people and tempt me to forget what service to God usually requires: faithfulness, and often of the long-suffering kind ....

Our walk with the Lord is very much like breathing. We are sustained by a steady, long-term process, rather than short bursts of hyperventilation.[21]

The Bible says, "Moreover it is required in stewards that one be found faithful" (1 Corinthians 4:2). One day when we stand before God in heaven, He's going to welcome us home.

He will not say, "Welcome home good and successful servant" or "Welcome home good and famous servant." No, heaven's badge of honor is faithfulness. One day God will say, "Welcome home good and faithful servant."

Christ Is at the Center of It All

Finally, and greatest of all, the book of Colossians tells us Christ is at the center of it all. Notice how many times the name Christ appears, just in the first paragraph of this letter!

Paul was an apostle of Jesus Christ (Colossians 1:1); the saints were faithful brethren in Christ (Colossians 1:2); grace and peace are from the Lord Jesus Christ (Colossians 1:2); we give thanks to the God and Father of our Lord Jesus Christ (Colossians 1:3); our faith is in the Lord Jesus Christ (Colossians 1:4); Epaphras was a faithful minister of Christ (Colossians 1:7).

This letter to the Colossians is a Christ-centered letter.

This whole story started when Paul preached the Gospel in Ephesus. Epaphras and Philemon heard the Gospel and carried it back to their little city where they established a church. Philemon opened his home to the church. Archippus became the pastor of that church, and Epaphras loved the church enough to get arrested in Rome while trying to get Paul's help to keep it healthy.

The glorious drama of the Church is always the story of people working together, facing challenges, trusting God and moving forward. The Gospel is not static but dynamic. The stories of the Gospel could not be manufactured. The Gospel of Jesus Christ changes everything.

Our family enjoys attending the San Diego Padres baseball games. We were so excited for the 2021 season we got seats right on the field behind first base. These seats come with a package of all the food you can eat. It's not free, but since we pay for it upfront, it seems like it's free. My two grandsons, David Todd and Bradley, think it's free and I promise you the Padres are losing money on them.

Where our seats are located, a certain woman serves food to everyone in that section. Her name is Debra, and she's a very hard worker. She takes good care of those two boys and all of us.

Because of other demands, I wasn't able to go to any of the early season games, but in August my friend Jack Graham came to San Diego for vacation. I promised to take him to a game.

During the game while Jack was up talking to some other people, Debra came over and sat down in the seat beside me. She said, "Are you the real David Jeremiah?"

I told her I was the only one I knew.

She told me she had recently gotten out of prison. While in prison, someone had given her a copy of the *Turning Points* magazine. She said she read it from cover to cover in one sitting, and when she got to the end of the magazine where the Gospel was presented, she accepted Jesus Christ as her Savior. It changed her life and she wanted to thank me.

I accepted her gratitude, but I realized I was just a part of the many people who make that magazine possible. It wasn't me who had changed her life, but the many faithful men and women who created that beautiful magazine and the many who circulate it and pray for us and support us.

And most of all, it was Jesus—just Jesus!

Oh, how wonderful to be part of what our Lord is doing!

Oh, the power of the Gospel unto salvation!

CHAPTER 2

Wisdom and Understanding

COLOSSIANS 1:9-14

ALMOST ONE HUNDRED YEARS AGO A YOUNG MISSIONARY in Ecuador named V. Raymond Edman staggered in the jungle, desperately ill. "He'll be dead by morning," the doctor said. Edman's wife dyed her wedding dress black, readying it for the funeral, which, in the tropics, would take place quickly. A sense of shock and sorrow hung over their little home.

Thousands of miles away, Edman's friend, Dr. Joseph Evans, interrupted a prayer meeting, saying, "I feel we must pray for Raymond Edman in Ecuador." The group prayed earnestly, until Evans cried out, "Praise the Lord! The victory is won!" Edman recovered and went on to have a remarkable career. He eventually became president of Wheaton College and personally mentored hundreds of students including Billy Graham.

I don't know what happened to the black wedding dress, but I do know the story of the Church has been repeatedly dyed in golden hues by the power of intercessory prayer.[1]

Jesus Christ is our ultimate Intercessor (Romans 8:34; Hebrews 7:25). As He prays for us, we're to do the same, offering "supplications, prayers, intercessions, and giving of thanks" for other people (1 Timothy 2:1). The word "intercession" refers to the practice of praying for others. Our Lord closed the gap between us and God when He died on the cross. Because of His mediation, we can intercede in prayer on behalf of others, asking God to grant our requests according to His will.

Intercessory prayer isn't for super-Christians who are called to a specific ministry of intercession. We're all intercessors! It's part of your calling in Christ. What a privilege to come boldly before the throne of Almighty God with the ability to influence others by the arc of your prayers!

The Bible tells us to offer intercessory prayers for: those in authority (1 Timothy 2:2); Jerusalem (Psalm 122:6); friends (Job 42:8); fellow countrymen (Romans 10:1); the sick (James 5:14); our enemies (Jeremiah 29:7); those who persecute us (Matthew 5:44); those who forsake us (2 Timothy 4:16); and all people (1 Timothy 2:1).

Can you create your own prayer list from those items? Can you become an intercessor? You'll find all you need to begin in Colossians 1:9-14, where the apostle Paul models intercessory prayer for us. His prayer is a pattern for how we should pray for others.

Three aspects of intercessory prayer stand out to me in this passage—its persistence, its petitions, and its possibilities. Let me show you.

The Persistence of Paul's Prayer

Colossians teaches us to pray without ceasing; that is, without getting discouraged and quitting. Paul's prayers for the Colossians were tireless and ceaseless. By the time he wrote this letter, he had possibly been praying for this church for nearly a decade!

In Luke 11, Jesus told of a man who went to his neighbor's house at midnight, needing food for an unexpected guest. The neighbor answered back, presumably in a loud whisper, saying he couldn't get out of bed. In those days, people slept in one room, and his children had finally gone to sleep on either side of him, even the fussiest. But the man kept knocking until the neighbor threw off the covers and gave him all the bread he wanted. It was the man's persistence that opened the door.

The Lord said, "And so I tell you, keep on asking, and you will receive what you ask for. Keep on seeking, and you will find. Keep on knocking, and the door will be opened to you" (Luke 11:9, NLT).

A few chapters later, in Luke 18, Jesus told a similar story about a persistent woman who gained her request because of her perseverance. The lesson in that passage: We "should always pray and never give up" (Luke 18:1, NLT).

This isn't the easiest habit to learn. Many of us fail to pray as we should, but there are ways of weaving this habit into the rhythms of our lives.

Emma Daniel Gray worked for the federal government as a charwoman, which is an old word for *cleaning woman*. She started in 1943, and for over a decade she cleaned various government agencies in Washington. In 1955, she was transferred to the White House. For the next twenty-four years she diligently cleaned the West Wing. Every day when she came to the president's chair, she paused, cleaning materials in hand, and prayed. She asked for blessings, wisdom, and safety for each of the six presidents she served.[2]

Emma's prayers weren't long or complex, but they were persistent. She prayed faithfully over a period of decades. Have you prayed for someone or something as consistently as that? Don't stop! John Wesley advised, "Storm the throne of grace and persevere there, and mercy will come down."

Yes, it will!

The Petition of Paul's Prayer

Our next lesson from Paul's intercessory example has to do with his petitions—what he prayed when he prayed for the Colossians.

I've lived long enough to have heard some strange prayer requests. I read about one pastor who got a note from a child asking for prayer for the boy's pet scorpion. Another child put this request on a prayer hotline: "Please pray that my mother will not be allergic to cats. I want a cat, but I really hate to ask my mother to move out."

I'll pray for almost anything a child requests! But as people mature—as we all mature—our prayers should grow deeper and wiser. Paul gives us great insights into that. His prayer for the Colossians actually began back in verse 3: "We give thanks to the God and Father of our Lord Jesus Christ, praying always for you."

He kept praying all the way to verse fourteen, but in my opinion, his key petition is in verse 9: "That you may be filled with the knowledge of His will in all wisdom and spiritual understanding."

He begged God to fill the Colossians with the knowledge of His will in all wisdom and spiritual understanding. Those are some big concepts, but try praying those qualities into someone for whom you are troubled. You might want to pause right now, think of a troubled loved one, and say: "Lord, fill him or her with the knowledge of Your will in all wisdom and spiritual understanding."

Believe me, that's a powerful prayer.

Let's break it down a bit. Remember, the Colossians were battling a Gnostic heresy. The original Greek word in verse 9 for "knowledge" is *epignosis*, which conveys the idea of full and accurate knowledge. Paul wanted to replace the danger of false ideas creeping into the minds of the Christians. He wanted God to fill them with true knowledge.

Dr. A. T. Robertson wrote: "The antidote for the false claim to knowledge (*gnosis*) by the Gnostics is *additional* knowledge (*epignosis*)—richer knowledge, true knowledge, knowledge directed toward the true God who makes His will known."[3]

The knowledge Paul desired for the Colossians included biblical wisdom. Someone has defined wisdom as "knowledge using its head." To have knowledge with wisdom is to be able to perform what you know, to live it out, and to make it practical.

Knowledge doesn't always translate into wisdom and understanding. Maybe you know someone who has lots of knowledge but little wisdom. It reminds me of the man who had so many degrees he no longer had a temperature!

We all know smart people who have difficulty navigating the simplicities of the everyday. For example, one person wrote, "My brother-in-law is a pretty clever guy. But one day he started a bath for his kid and couldn't get the water to turn off. In a panic, he called a plumber friend asking him to come quickly or the house would flood. His friend said, 'Could you just pull the plug?'"[4]

We've all done foolish things in a panic, but when wisdom and understanding catches up with knowledge, we're more likely to stay calm and carry on. The link between knowledge and wisdom is critical because it bridges the gap between what we *know* and what we *do*—between what we claim to believe and how we actually behave. Some Christians are filled with knowledge, but it seldom affects the way they live. It doesn't dawn on them that their knowledge should inform their behavior.

Oh, that you would make this a prayer towards those for whom you're burdened—"Lord, fill them with the knowledge of Your will in all wisdom and spiritual understanding."

The Possibilities of Paul's Prayer

For the rest of the chapter, I want to talk about the possibilities of prayer, unfolding this entire passage and looking at the specific things the Lord can do in those who are filled with the knowledge of His will. And remember, whenever you're not sure what to pray for someone for whom you're burdened, you can turn to this passage, put his or her name in it, and turn it into a personal intercession that you'll never wear out.

Let's track five enormous realities through these verses.

We Can Please God Continuously

First, when we're filled with spiritual understanding, we'll "walk worthy of the Lord, fully pleasing Him" (Colossians 1:10). This is personal. This is about pleasing God. Think of someone you strive to please and you'll understand.

After Donna and I were married, we planted a church in Fort Wayne, Indiana, and we built a house across the street from the church. In the early days, we had no staff and I worked long hours. On one occasion, we had a dinner appointment with friends. We had hired a babysitter, and I told Donna I'd be home just in time for us to make our engagement, so she should be ready for the evening.

It was a cold winter's evening in Fort Wayne. I warmed up the car, pulled into the driveway of our little home, and beeped the horn. I thought Donna would pop out of the front door, but she didn't come! I waited until I couldn't wait any longer, then I got out and went to find her.

Donna was sitting on the living room couch with her coat buttoned up, her scarf around her neck, and her arms folded across her chest. She looked at me and said, "I don't respond to beeps."

I learned that day what *did* and *did not* please my wife, and I can honestly say I've never beeped for her again in nearly fifty years. The better you know someone, the better you know what pleases them. That includes knowing God! There are little ways every day to please Him, and we're to find them. Ephesians 5:10 says, "And find out what pleases the Lord" (NIV).

Colossians 1:10 says He is pleased when we "walk worthy" of Him.

Paul said something similar three other times in his writings:

- "Walk worthy of the calling with which you were called" (Ephesians 4:1).

- "Let your conduct be worthy of the gospel of Christ" (Philippians 1:27).

- "Walk worthy of God who calls you into His own kingdom and glory" (1 Thessalonians 2:12).

When we study God's Word, we develop an understanding of what truly pleases Him. This knowledge enables us to "walk worthy of God" by putting it into practice. I like what the old Bible teacher C. F. D. Moule said: pleasing God refers "to the meeting of His wishes, so as to not only obey explicit precepts, but ... to anticipate in everything, His will."[5]

We Can Produce Fruit Constantly

If the people we pray for are being filled with the knowledge of God's will, growing in wisdom, pleasing Him, and walking worthy of Him, they'll soon be "fruitful in every good work" (Colossians 1:10). That's the next thing to pray about.

What does it mean to bear fruit? I've found five New Testament examples of fruit-bearing where the word "fruit" is used in the text.

First, Galatians 5:22-23 uses the word "fruit" to describe our *character*—those godly character traits that should be growing in our lives: "But the fruit of the Spirit is love, joy, peace, long suffering, kindness, goodness, faithfulness, gentleness, self-control."

Jay Blossom said that when he was a child in children's church, his teachers told him "an elaborate story about a peace-loving pirate named Long John, who watched over the ship of a virtuous sea captain named Sir Charles." The pirate exhibited all the elements of the fruit of the Spirit, and the story was summed up with a closing sentence, which the class learned: "Long John, peaceful pirate, keeps guard for gentle Sir Charles."

Jay has never forgotten that sentence because that's how he learned the fruit of the Spirit. Each word of the sentence started with the first letter of the qualities listed: "L ... J ... P ... P ... K ... G ... F ... G ... SC."

Jay wrote, "'Long John, peaceful pirate' has helped me to remember that gentleness, peace, kindness and joy are not just culturally contextual values, but are gifts from God and outgrowths of the Holy Spirit's working in my life. My goal is to create room for that fruit to thrive. Because I'm confident of this very thing: God, who hath begun a good work in me, will perform it until the day of Jesus Christ (Philippians 1:6)."[6]

Let's pray "Long John" into the hearts of our loved ones!

Second, the *conduct* of our lives is a kind of fruit. Romans 6:22 says, "But now having been set free from sin, and having become slaves of God, you have your fruit to holiness."

We don't have to be perfect, but as we grow in the perfections of Christ, He uses us even when we think we're failing. I read a story about a servant who carried two large pots, each at the end of a pole across his neck. One of the pots was cracked. At the end of the long walk from the stream to home, the cracked pot arrived only half full. The other pot was perfect and always delivered a full portion of water.

The perfect pot was proud of its accomplishments, but the cracked pot was ashamed of its imperfection and miserable over accomplishing only half of what it had been made to do. One day the cracked pot spoke to the servant by the stream. "I am ashamed of myself, and I want to apologize to you. For these past two years I've been able to deliver only half my load because this crack in my side causes water to leak out all the way home."

The servant said, "As we return home, I want you to notice the beautiful flowers along the path." As they went up the hill, the cracked pot noticed the wildflowers on the side of the path. When they reached the house, the servant said to the pot, "Did you notice the flowers grew only on your side of the path, not on the other pot's side? That's because I have always known about your flaw, and I took advantage of it. I planted flower seeds on your side of the path, and every day while we walk back from the stream, you watered them."[7]

The Bible says, "This beautiful treasure [the Gospel] is contained in us—cracked pots made of earth and clay—so that the transcendent character of this power may be clearly seen as coming from God and not from us" (2 Corinthians 4:7, VOICE).

We bear fruit through our conduct.

Third, the Bible speaks of our *conversation* and words of thanksgiving and praise as the fruit of our lips (Hebrews 13:15). When we sing, praise, and glorify God, it's the fruit of worship, which pleases God. Have you discovered the power of the classic hymns in helping your mind stay fresh when you awaken in the morning? Now that we have downloadable music accessible on our phones, try listening to "O, for a Thousand Tongues" as you shower, shave, or put on your makeup. You'll find yourself singing along. That pleases the Lord, and the whole day starts differently.

Fourth, the concept of fruit in the Bible sometimes describes our monetary *contributions* to God. Paul told the Philippians: "For even in Thessalonica you sent aid once and again for my necessities. Not that I seek the gift, but I seek the fruit that abounds to your account" (Philippians 4:16-17).

When we fund God's work, that's another evidence of being fruitful. According to a survey in October 2021, only thirteen percent of American Protestant evangelicals give a tenth of their income to the Lord, and, even more shocking, a good half of all American Christians give less than one percent to the cause of Christ.[8] If I owned an orchard that produced such meager fruit, I'd wonder if the trees were diseased.

As we grow in knowledge and in the wisdom of Christ, we become fruitful givers. We rejoice in worshiping God with our tithes and offerings.

Fifth, the Bible speaks of the *converts* we win to the Lord as fruit. Proverbs 11:30 says, "The fruit of the righteous is a tree of life, and he who wins souls is wise." Paul called the new believers in Achaia "firstfruits" because they were the first of many in that area who were coming to Christ (1 Corinthians 16:15). Whenever we're planting Gospel seed, we're leading to a harvest.

Early in my ministry, I had the opportunity to lead a certain man to Jesus Christ. One night a few months later he called me at one o'clock in the morning. "Pastor," he said, "This is Gene McCoy. Congratulations. You're a grandfather!"

I said, "What?"

"Yeah, it's true. You're a grandfather. You know, you led me to Christ a few months ago, and today I led a young lady to Christ. And since you're my spiritual father, I guess that makes you her spiritual grandfather."

It took a moment to catch on at that wee hour. But he was right! When we're Christians reproducing ourselves in the lives of others, we're being fruitful.

Now, think of how your prayers can begin to prompt these things in the life of someone else! As they grow in knowledge and spiritual wisdom, according to your requests for them, they can begin to please God continually and produce fruit constantly.

If we just stopped there, we'd be successful. But there's more!

We Can Progress in Knowledge Consistently

According to verse 10, those for whom we pray can progress in knowledge consistently. Paul prayed that the Colossians would "walk worthy of the Lord, fully pleasing Him, being fruitful in every good work *and increasing in the knowledge of God*" (emphasis added). When Kent Hughes studied this passage, he observed:

> Paul saw the dynamic connection between action and knowledge. He knew that as they "continued bearing every good work," they would naturally open themselves to "growing in the knowledge of God." One begets the other in a delectable upward spiral: the more one truly serves Him, the more one opens to knowledge of Him—the more one knows of Him, the more one wants to serve. So it goes onward and upward![9]

While most of the rest of the world is in a downward spiral, those for whom we pray can reverse course and travel in the upward spiral of knowing Jesus better and better and drawing from His strength more and more.

We Can Persevere Under Pressure Cheerfully

As a result, we and those for whom we're praying can persevere under pressure cheerfully. Look at Paul's prayer again. He asked God to fill the Colossians with the knowledge of His will with all spiritual understanding "that you may walk worthy of the Lord, fully pleasing Him, being fruitful in every good work and increasing in the knowledge of God;

strengthened with all might, according to His glorious power, for all patience and longsuffering with joy" (Colossians 1:10-11, emphasis added).

Wow! One thing leads to another. When you pray for someone, it triggers a domino effect of grace in their lives, leading to their ability to persevere under pressure cheerfully.

Beth Loggans exhibited this. She's a wife, mother, and grandmother who was diagnosed in 2018 with acute lymphocytic leukemia, a fast-spreading form of blood cancer. The news came as a terrible shock, of course. At one point, the chemotherapy sent her into liver failure. Her doctors told her she had a small chance of surviving. Then came a bone marrow transplant, which involved many trips to a Detroit hospital.

What's truly incredible is Beth's attitude. She told her local newspaper, "I have so much to be thankful for. I am thankful that God brought me through this and am thankful to the Lord Jesus Christ for his comfort and his calming of my fears .... I am thankful for my family and the people I have met because of my illness, the doctors, nurses, fellow patients and their families. I am thankful for the prayers of the people from many churches, people I don't even know."

She also said, "I determined to choose joy. I'd say to anybody in a similar situation, 'Choose joy.'"[10]

Imagine how many people were interceding for Beth! She's a walking example of Colossians 1:11: "Strengthened with all might, according to His glorious power, for all patience and longsuffering with joy."

In the past, when I've seen words in the Bible like *power* and *might* and *strength*, I've thought, *That's for the big test. When*

I have to stand up against some daunting problem, like that faced by Beth. Yes, but I've also been learning we need strength, not just for the momentary challenges, but for the long haul. The Christian life isn't a hundred-yard dash. It's a marathon!

Paul's prayer for the patience and endurance of the Colossian believers was tied to his understanding of the challenges they were facing. Ralph P. Martin said, "Endurance is in reference to adverse circumstances; patience is in reference to difficult people."[11]

The Colossians were facing both, and so are we! Oh, how we need to ask God to give one another patience and longsuffering with joy. Each of those words is important. An expositor of the past wrote, "Patience and longsuffering without joy are apt to be cold and unattractive .... But when patience and longsuffering are permeated by joyfulness, the very life of Christ is lived over again in His followers."[12]

We Can Praise God Correctly

The apostle Paul wasn't finished in telling us what prayer can do. He went on to suggest another possible result of intercession—the ability to praise God correctly. Verse 12 says, "Giving thanks to the Father" (Colossians 1:12).

That brings us all the way back to the praise and thanksgiving with which the prayer began in verse 3. If you study verses 12 through 14 carefully, you'll see how Paul settles into his theme, giving us four great reasons for praise. Look at the verses: "Giving thanks to the Father who has qualified us to be partakers of the inheritance of the saints in the light. He has delivered us from the power of darkness and conveyed us into the kingdom of the Son of His love, in whom we have redemption through His blood, the forgiveness of sins."

In my notes, I outlined these verses like this.

He Remade Us

First, we thank God because He remade us. He "qualified us to be partakers of the inheritance of the saints in the light" (Colossians 1:12). God remade us so we can claim our inheritance, "the inheritance of the saints in the light." Because we've been remade, we're now able to live for God in the darkness of this world. One day our heavenly inheritance will be fully realized, but for now we live in the joys of its preview and in the awareness of the pardoning grace of God.

Diane Komp, a pediatric oncologist, tells a remarkable story of the way God can remake us. One day the doctor took a call from a woman who shared something very heavy. The woman said that in the early years of her marriage, she had an affair and became pregnant. When this new lover learned about her pregnancy, he gave her a pill to swallow in hopes of inducing an abortion. It didn't work, and he left her. The woman returned to her husband, and he forgave her, and together they celebrated when the baby, whom they named Arthur, was born.

But three years later, Arthur developed cancer. And over the next five years, the boy had multiple relapses and almost died on many occasions.

The mother's question to the oncologist that day was: "Do you think that the concoction I drank to abort the pregnancy caused the cancer?"

Imagine the nagging, torturing guilt behind that question!

Dr. Komp responded by saying that was a question she could not answer—there was no way to know what caused the cancer.

Arthur's mother later explained to Dr. Komp that she had grown up in a church that preached forgiveness. Nevertheless, she had never been able to forgive herself and had rejected God's forgiveness. But one day she underlined every passage in her Bible that referred to God's forgiveness and was amazed that the burden was finally lifted.

"The healing of memories and guilt can sometimes be more difficult than healing cancer," says Dr. Komp. But with God, nothing is impossible!

Eventually, Arthur received a new experimental drug, and miracuolously it worked! Years later, the mother called Dr. Komp again. This time she invited her to Arthur's wedding, and what a celebration it was![13]

In this difficult case, there were two healings—one from cancer and the other from cancerous guilt. No one goes through life without regrets, but everything changes when we realize how God remakes us! He qualifies us through Christ to be partakers with His saints in the kingdom of light. Imagine how your prayers for someone today can heighten this awareness and herald this praise.

He Rescued Us

Paul continued, "He has delivered us from the power of darkness" (Colossians 1:13). This deliverance is not an ongoing process but a definite event in history. The tense here is past. It has already happened. When Christ died for us on the cross,

He rendered Satan's power over us null and void. We've been delivered from the power of darkness and never need to be dominated by error and confusion. What a reminder for the Colossians as Gnosticism was swirling around their heads. And what a reminder for us as we try to negotiate our mixed-up world!

Someone you know needs to praise God for His rescue and recovery efforts. Oh, pray that they will see it and worship our Rescuer and Redeemer!

He Relocated Us

We also need to pray that others will praise God because He has relocated us. He "conveyed us into the kingdom of the Son of His love" (Colossians 1:13). The word translated "conveyed" is the picture of an eastern conqueror who uprooted his vanquished enemies and carried them away to another place. In other words, God has removed us from Satan's sphere of darkness and relocated us in His own Kingdom which is the Kingdom of the Son of His love.

Recently a young man in Mexico told his story. As a boy, he lived in squalor with his baby brother, mother, and her boyfriend. His mother scavenged for items to sell in order to buy food. One day, she came upon a little box of books—New Testaments, published by the Gideons International. The boy, named Fermin, began reading one of the books. He loved the sections in the back that told him where to turn in the Bible for "Help in Time of Need." Those little books changed the boy forever, and later his mother also came to Christ. His mom's life stabilized, and she became a cook in a hotel. They were able to buy a house and relocate.[14]

Their great relocation, however, wasn't from a shack to a house; it was from the darkness to the kingdom of light.

He Redeemed Us

All this happens because, as Paul told the Colossians, we have been redeemed. He wrote: "In whom we have redemption through His blood, the forgiveness of sins" (Colossians 1:14).

To redeem someone means "to buy them back and set them free." Jesus' death was the price necessary to buy us back and set us free from sin. Because of His death and resurrection, we're set free from both the penalty and the power of sin.

Not long ago, Lee Horton was released from prison after 25 years behind bars. In an interview with National Public Radio, he tried to explain the sense of joy and freedom that comes when one leaves prison. He said,

Everything becomes beautiful to you.

When I got out, I went to the DMV a couple of days later to get my license back. And I stood in line for two and a half hours. And I heard all the stories that everybody tells us, the bad things about the DMV. But I had the most beautiful time. And all the people were looking at me because I was smiling and laughing, and they couldn't understand why I was so happy. Just being in that line was a beautiful thing.

One of my morning rituals every morning is I send a message of good morning to every one of my contacts. And that's, like, 42 people .... I send them good morning, good morning, good morning. Have a nice day. And they're like, how long can I keep doing this? But they don't understand that I was deprived. And now, it's like I have been released, and I've been reborn into a better day, into a new day. Like, the person I was no longer exists. And I've stepped through that time machine. I've stepped through the looking glass onto the other side, and everything is beautiful. And even people getting upset to me seems to be very nice .... I like to just look at people now. And I smile, and I ask myself, do they know what my secret is?[15]

That's something of how we should feel as the redeemed of the Lord! He remade us, rescued us, relocated us, and redeemed us. He is our freedom! It's easy to take our blessings for granted, but that was why Paul was always praying for his friends. He wanted them to experience the full joy of their salvation. He wanted the Gospel to mean more and more to them with each passing day.

That's why he has given us this unfolding prayer to offer for ourselves and others. If it was good enough for him to pray for the Colossians, it's a great prayer for you to pray into your own life—and to use as a pattern as you intercede for the people God places on your heart.

I began this chapter with a story about intercessory prayer involving a missionary named V. Raymond Edman. Let me end with another missionary story.

In 1908, James Fraser gave up a promising engineering career to become a missionary to the Lisuland of China, in the foothills of the Himalayas. This area was very remote, and Fraser had trouble working with these people when winter snows made it too dangerous for him to gather them together in church services.

He grew very frustrated when his plans to visit the Lisu church were hindered again and again. But he became convinced God was *in* the problem—it was a challenge of the Lord's own making.

Fraser worked out it would take him three to five days to conduct church services in the highland villages of Lisuland. It required one or two days of travel up into the mountains, a day of gathering together, and then one or two days for the return trip. He decided to try an experiment. "What would happen if I decided to spend the time that I would have spent gathering with these Lisu people praying for them instead?"

Fraser committed to his experiment completely. In snowy weather, he prayed for the highland villagers for three to five days instead of visiting them. Once the spring sun had melted the snow, he climbed the mountains to discover what had happened.

Fraser's converts in the highland villages had prospered during the winter months when he was unable to gather with them. Because of their Bible reading and isolated prayer times, the believers in the highlands of Lisuland had grown far more during the winter than the Christians in the lowlands—those he had been busy visiting and gathering with all winter long.

From that day on, he was determined never to fret when he could not gather people, but always to seize it as a God-given invitation to pray for people instead.

And by the way, today there are about 935,000 Lisu in Southern China and more than 400,000 are Christians![16]

V. Raymond Edman, the apostle Paul, and James Fraser were all convinced of the power of intercessory prayer. How about you? Take up Paul's prayer in Colossians 1:9-14 and make it your own.

Ask God to give you the name of someone for whom you can pray and then put their name in Colossians 1! Who knows what the Lord will do in the lives of others as you pray on their behalf!

CHAPTER 3

The Fullness of Christ

COLOSSIANS 1:15-23

FOR THOUSANDS OF PEOPLE, IT WAS THE TRIP OF A lifetime—the chance to attend a World's Fair and see the newest inventions, the greatest spectacles (including the original Ferris wheel), and exhibits from 46 countries in the world. The 1893 World's Columbian Exposition covered nearly 700 acres, and millions of people streamed into Chicago by rail, by boat, on horses, and in carriages.

Evangelist D. L. Moody, whose ministry was based in Chicago, instantly saw the possibilities the World's Fair afforded evangelism. He recruited, trained, and commissioned workers to share the Gospel, and he assigned preachers to occupy preaching posts throughout the city. He used churches and rented theaters, and he erected a circus tent to preach the Word.

Among the features of the Columbian Exposition was the World's Parliament of Religions, where representatives of the world's religions met to share their best points and perhaps come up with a new world religion. Moody's friends wanted him to attack the meeting, but Moody wouldn't be distracted from his own soul-winning endeavors.

He said, "I am going to make Jesus Christ so attractive that men will turn to Him."

Moody knew that preaching Christ as preeminent—the peerless, supreme, all-sufficient Christ, clearly presented—would do the job. And it did! "The Chicago campaign of 1893 is considered the greatest evangelistic work of Moody's celebrated life, and thousands came to Christ."[1]

The next passage we're approaching in Colossians is a powerfully-reasoned presentation about the preeminence of Jesus Christ. The apostle Paul felt, as Moody later did, that nothing can attack error like the clear presentation of the glory and supremacy of Christ. The best defense is a good offense.

That's still true. In all things, Christ must have the preeminence!

Every biblical scholar who studies the life of Jesus understands there are two great sides of this truth. We must understand our Lord's Person and His work—who He is and what He does. In Colossians 1:15-20, Paul tackled the first of these, and he dealt with the second in verses 21-23.

Let's dig in!

The Person of Jesus Christ: Who He Is

"He is the image of the invisible God, the firstborn over all creation. For by Him all things were created that are in heaven and that are on earth, visible and invisible, whether thrones or dominions or principalities or powers. All things were created through Him and for Him. And He is before all things, and in Him all things consist" (Colossians 1:15-17).

That paragraph is rich enough to fill a book, isn't it? But for the sake of space I want to show you three special relationships that help us define the identity of Christ—His relationship with His Father, with His creation, and with His Church.

In Relation to the Father

Let's start with one word: *invisible*. Colossians 1:15 says Jesus "is the image of the invisible God." Invisibility is something that intrigues us even as children. One little girl, when she got into trouble, thought if she tightly squeezed her eyes closed, she'd be invisible. Writers of fantasy and science fiction take advantage of our fascination with invisibility by weaving it into their plots. There are moments when we all wish we could be invisible.

But is invisibility scientifically possible?

For years, scientists have been postulating mathematical formulas that could theoretically create invisible cloaks by bending light rays around objects, rendering them invisible to the eye. But much of the research is for military purposes, and so far we haven't seen if it really works.

Nevertheless, invisibility is real. The Bible clearly teaches that when God created the visible realm He also created the unseen realm. Paul wrote in this passage, "For by Him all things were created that are in heaven and that are on earth, *visible and invisible*" (Colossians 1:16, emphasis added).

Almighty God the Father is Himself invisible. Colossians 1:15 describes Him as "the invisible God." In 1 Timothy 1:17, Paul said, "Now to the King eternal, immortal, invisible, to God who alone is wise, be honor and glory forever and ever. Amen."

John wrote, "No one has seen God at any time" (1 John 4:12).

But in his Gospel, John also said: "No one has ever seen God, but the one and only Son, who is himself God and is in closest relationship with the Father, has made him known" (John 1:18, NIV).

This is precisely what Paul is affirming in Colossians 1:15. Many theologians believe even in heaven we will not visibly see God the Father, but we will see Jesus, for Revelation 22:4 says, "They shall see His face."

Jesus Christ, then, is the image of the invisible God. He is God made visible to us, the manifestation of the Divine nature.

The word translated "image" is *eikon.* Dr. Lloyd John Ogilvie explained, "An eikon was a representation, or reproduction with precise likeness, derived exactly from the prototype. An image of a sovereign or hero on a coin, or a painted portrait of a person's likeness, was an eikon .... The word *eikon* also means 'manifestation, an observable exhibition.' What Paul wanted to establish was that Jesus was the exact likeness of God."[2]

In this passage, Paul was turning the tables on the false teachers. They taught that Jesus, if He was a god, was one of the lesser gods. But Paul insisted Jesus was not simply a lesser god of some sort. He was the God—the true image of the true God, the visible manifestation of the invisible King.

A chapter later, Paul added: "For in Him dwells all the fullness of the Godhead bodily" (Colossians 2:9). The word "fullness" is the Greek word *pleroma*, meaning, "full fullness." In other words, there is no part of God that is missing in Jesus. He is God Himself, the very God of God. He is not almost God or a little less than God. He is fully God, the fullness of God bodily, the visible manifestation of the invisible God.

John Phillips wrote, "What God is, Jesus is. What God does, He does. What God says, He says. There is not one iota of difference between God in Heaven and Jesus on earth."

Let that sink in! Phillips went on to say, "For thirty-three and a half years, the Lord Jesus lived on this planet as Man inhabited by God. He set before us a flawless, moment-by-moment, audiovisual, full-color, three-dimensional demonstration of what God is like. He was [and is] 'the image of the invisible God.'"[3]

Believe me, my friend, when you realize that Jesus Christ of Nazareth is and always will be God, the true God, very God, and the eternal God in everything, it answers a lot of questions, lifts a lot of burdens, and solves a lot of problems.

Pastor D. James Kennedy said in a sermon, "I remember years ago talking to a man in his home about Christ and asking him who he thought Jesus was. He said, 'Oh, He's a wonderful man. He was the greatest man who ever lived, the most loving and gracious person who ever walked upon this earth.'"

"I said, 'Let me tell you something I believe will startle you. According to the Scriptures, and the historic Christian faith, Jesus of Nazareth, the carpenter of Galilee was and is the eternal Creator of the universe, the omnipotent, omniscient, and Almighty God.'

"Instantly, his eyes filled with tears and this man of about fifty-five or sixty said, 'I have been in church all my life and I never heard that before. But I have always thought that is the way it ought to be—that God ought to be like Jesus.'"[4]

That is the way it ought to be—and that is how it is!

In Relation to All Creation

Let's go on to the next part of verse 15: "He is the image of the invisible God, the firstborn over all creation."

Jesus is the firstborn over all creation. The word "firstborn" bothers a lot of people, and even today false teachers try to use this verse to claim Jesus was the first created object in history.

Scholarship on this subject is clear. The word "firstborn" in this context implies Jesus is the supreme Head of creation and not a created entity.

The word *first* has two distinct senses, both in Greek and English. It may mean "first in time" or it may mean "first in rank." When we say Neil Armstrong was the first person to walk on the moon, we mean first in terms of time. When we call the President's wife the "First Lady," we mean first in terms of rank. She's the wife of the President. When a child wins first prize in a competition, it refers to their status and accomplishment.

In the Bible, the firstborn was typically heir of all, so the term "firstborn" came to mean the head, leader, or supreme one. For example, Psalm 89:27 says about David and his seed, "I will make him My firstborn, the highest of the kings of the earth."

Here the word "firstborn" is synonymous for the highest of all the kings—the King of kings. Since Jesus existed before creation, He is exalted above creation. Paul wanted to convey to the Colossians that Christ was not only uncreated; He is Himself the Creator. Jesus Christ, who is the visible image of the invisible God, is the firstborn over all creation because He is the Creator of all creation. He is the heir of all.

Jesus is the creator of all creation. Colossians 1:16 and 17 go on to say, "For by Him all things were created that are in heaven and that are on earth, visible and invisible, whether thrones or dominions or principalities or powers. All things were created through Him and for Him. And He is before all things, and in Him all things consist."

Four times in these two verses, Paul uses the expression "all things," stressing that Jesus Christ is the Creator of the whole universe. The word *universe* doesn't occur in the Bible, but the phrase "all things" encompasses the universe and beyond. Jesus is preeminent over all things, for He created it all.

Hebrews 1:2, echoes these words: "[God] has in these last days spoken to us by His Son ... through whom also He made the worlds."

The apostle John opened his Gospel on the same note: "In the beginning was the Word, and the Word was with God, and the Word was God. He was in the beginning with God. *All things* were made through Him, and without Him nothing was made that was made" (John 1:1-3, emphasis added).

Even the famous neo-atheist Richard Dawkins has trouble denying the marvel of an intelligently-designed creation. In a tweet, he said he was "[knocked] ... sideways with wonder at the miniaturized intricacy of the data-processing machinery in the living cell." Dawkins is not about to admit the living cell is actually created by a personal God. He simply is overwhelmed at its microscopic design and precision.

I'm overwhelmed too, but I'm also filled with worship toward Him who created everything from a tiny cell to the galaxies beyond our gaze.

Jesus is the goal of creation. Our Lord Jesus Christ is not only the God of creation; He is the goal of creation. Colossians 1:16 says, "All things were created through Him and for Him." The same thought is found in Romans 11:36: "For of Him and through Him and to Him are all things, to whom be glory forever. Amen."

Some translate the word "for" with the word *toward*. This is even more astounding: "All things were created by Him and toward Him." In other words, everything begins with Him and ends with Him.

All things sprang forth at His command, and all things will return to Him at His command. Does this remind you of what Jesus said in Revelation 1:8? "'I am the Alpha and the Omega, the Beginning and the End,' says the Lord, 'who is and who was and who is to come, the Almighty.'"

Jesus is the predecessor of all creation. He is also the predecessor of all creation. "He is before all things" (Colossians 1:17). He existed when there was nothing except Father, Son, and Holy Spirit. When our Lord told His critics, "Before Abraham was, I AM," in John 8:58, they were flabbergasted. He was only in His thirties, and humanly speaking His statement seemed ridiculous. But it wasn't, for His eternal existence preceded His birth in Bethlehem.

He is the eternal I AM!

One of the most poignant biblical statements about our Lord's preexistence came from His own lips in His great prayer in John 17, on the eve of His crucifixion:

> I have finished the work which You have given Me
> to do. And now, O Father, glorify Me together with
> Yourself, with the glory which I had with You before
> the world was …. Father, I desire that they also whom
> You gave Me may be with Me where I am, that they
> may behold My glory which You have given Me; for
> You loved Me before the foundation of the world
> (verses 4-5, 24).

In other words, since Jesus predates the world it would be no exaggeration for Him to say, "Before Abraham was, I AM" (John 8:58).

Jesus is the sustainer of all creation. Paul's great description of our Lord in Colossians continues to unfold. He next says our Lord is the sustainer of creation. Colossians 1:17 says, "In Him all things consist."

The writer of the book of Hebrews tells us that Jesus Christ is "upholding all things by the word of His power" (Hebrews 1:3). Jesus Christ sustains the universe, maintaining the power and balance necessary for life's existence and continuity. He is the Creator.

Robert Jastrow, who admits to being an agnostic in religious matters, wrote a book entitled, *God and the Astronomers.* In it, he tried to explain why modern scientists are so adamantly opposed to any kind of creationism:

> Why this strange reaction on the part of many
> scientists? I think part of the answer is that scientists
> cannot bear the thought of a natural phenomenon
> which cannot be explained, even with unlimited time
> and money .... For the scientist who has lived his
> faith in the power of reason, the story ends like a bad
> dream. He has scaled the mountains of ignorance;
> he is about to conquer the highest peak; as he pulls
> himself over the final rock, he is greeted by a band
> of theologians who have been sitting there for
> centuries.[5]

Former NFL coach and NBC analyst Tony Dungy and his wife, Lauren, wrote a book in which they said Jesus was the glue that held them together in their marriage. It reminds me of 1 John 1:7: "But if we walk in the light as He is in the light, we have fellowship with one another." Jesus is the glue that holds me together—and He's the glue that holds everything together. In Him all things consist.

Jesus is the reconciler of all creation. As we keep reading this incredible passage in Colossians, it takes a very personal turn. The Lord Jesus is the God and the goal of Creation, the predecessor and sustainer of it all; He is also the reconciler of all creation. Colossians 1:20 says, "And by Him to reconcile all things to Himself, by Him, whether things on earth or things in heaven, having made peace through the blood of His cross."

Notice it's not God who needs to be reconciled to creation. It's creation that needs to be reconciled to God. Only one Person is qualified to be the reconciler, and that's the Lord Jesus Christ.

Our personal reconciliation took nothing less than the death of God's Son. But this verse teaches that our personal reconciliation was only one part of the reconciliation of the cross. God through the death of Christ not only reconciles sinners to Himself, but the Scripture says that He reconciles "all things" to Himself. Because of sin, creation is out of sync, but because of what Jesus did on the cross, one day all creation will be reconciled. That doesn't mean there will be no judgment of sin. It means one day all things will be as they should, and it starts with each of us as we receive Christ as Savior.

Pastor Paul Daugherty in Oklahoma had the misfortune of losing his Bible. Unknown to him, it ended up in the hands of a man named Clayton, who found it at a homeless shelter and started reading it. The name P. Daugherty was stamped on the front cover. Clayton had no idea who Daugherty was, but he noticed all his notes, underlines, and scribbled thoughts. Clayton came to treasure the same verses.

One day Clayton bowed his head and received Jesus Christ as Savior. He was gloriously reconciled to God, and he wanted to meet the Bible's original owner. He tracked him down, learned he was a pastor, and visited his church.

Daugherty recalls, "He came to church ... and showed me the Bible and asked if I knew who's it was! It was my old Bible from middle & high school that I lost and hadn't seen in 15 years! God used my old messy scribbled in Bible to save this guy's life who now is saved, set free, and brought his whole family with kids to church tonight!"[6]

Only Jesus can reconcile us to God like that!

In Relation to the Church

Having defined Jesus Christ in terms of creation, Paul presses forward to define Him in terms of His Church. Let's continue with Colossians 1:18-20: "And He is the head of the body, the church, who is the beginning, the firstborn from the dead, that in all things He may have the preeminence. For it pleased the Father that in Him all the fullness should dwell, and by Him to reconcile all things to Himself, by Him, whether things on earth or things in heaven, having made peace through the blood of His cross."

Jesus is the Head of the Body!

One of the awful forms of execution throughout history—we believe the apostle Paul himself died in this way—was decapitation. The moment the head is severed from the body, everything dies. The body cannot live without its head. We can lose a limb or even a vital organ and live, but there's no life without the head. God created the human brain as the computer controlling the entire body.

Here in Colossians, Paul tells us the Church is like a Body with Jesus Christ as its Head. All Christians of all the ages comprise the Body. We all derive our life from the Head, and we become part of that Body by the baptizing work of the Holy Spirit: "By one Spirit we were all baptized into one body" (1 Corinthians 12:13). We function in response to the directions given to us by the Head of the Church.

The apostle uses two terms to describe Jesus Christ as the Head of the Body: "And He is the head of the body, the church, who is the beginning, the firstborn from the dead" (Colossians 1:18).

He is the beginning of the Church, and He is the firstborn from the dead.

At the beginning, Jesus originated life; and by His resurrection, He overcame death.

In verses 16-17 we're made aware of Jesus' preeminence over His creation, and now in verse 18 we are told He desires the same preeminence over His Church: "That in all things He may have the preeminence."

Much that's gone wrong with the Church today is the result of a poor connection between the Head and the Body. A careless view of Christ leads to a Christless view of faith.

That was the fear Epaphras and Paul had concerning the little church in Colossae. Because of the intrusion of false teachers, the Colossians were beginning to substitute questions about food and drink, Sabbaths, feast days. and new moons for the worship of Jesus Christ. They were replacing the Lord with visions and angel worship and traditions and asceticism. They were in danger of losing all power because they were cutting themselves off from the source of power. Again, a body severed from its head dies!

Someone far more eloquent than I am wrote these words:

When the church has been victorious in power and
had a cutting edge in society, it has been because she
has kept Jesus Christ at the center of her creed and

her members have been captivated by His greatness. They have realized that in Him are hid all the treasures of wisdom and knowledge. They have not relied on a philosophy of empty deceit, according to human tradition. They have not gloried in intellectual superiority. They have been rightly related to the Church's head.

In its vital hours, Christ has been the center of the Church's worship. He has received the adoration of believing hearts. If we would see the Church blessed in our days with vibrant spirituality, we must constantly build our churches on and around Jesus Christ.[7]

A missionary photographer recently wrote about his first post-Covid trip to Africa. He was sent to Zambia to record what happened when a group of missionaries showed the *Jesus Film*. Word spread through the villages, and some people walked seven hours to see it. Everyone waited for the sun to set, and then in the darkness the projector beamed the story of Christ onto a large screen attached to the side of a building. For two hours, people were transfixed by the story of Jesus. Imagine learning of Jesus for the first time at a moment like that!

"It doesn't matter who you are or where you live," said the photographer, who travels under the name Luke. "When you hear the gospel, whether for the first time or for the hundredth time, you must make a personal decision to accept Jesus as your Savior and Lord, or not."[8]

The Work of Jesus Christ: What He Does

Having set forth the Person of Christ, now Paul moves to the subject of His work and ministry. Here's a detail worth noting. In verses 15-20, Paul didn't use the second person pronoun "you" even once. But in verses 21-23, he used it five times to explain how the preeminence of Christ intersects the past, present, and future of our lives. Paul made all of this about me and about you: "And you, who once were alienated and enemies in your mind by wicked works, yet now He has reconciled in the body of His flesh through death, to present you holy, and blameless, and above reproach in His sight" (verses 21-22).

He Has Reconciled You (Jesus and Your Past)

Increasing numbers of people are recognizing our ultimate human need is to be reconciled—we were enemies with God in our minds. We need to be reconciled with God through the death and sacrifice of Jesus.

Actor Nathaniel Buzolic has made it big in Hollywood acting in *Hacksaw Ridge* and other movies. Yet if you follow his social media, you'll find he's far more interested in someone else—the Lord Jesus.

Recently Buzolic posted a picture of the Sea of Galilee and said that while Jesus healed the sick during the days of His ministry, "What is far more important than a physical healing was a renewal of the mind. To be transformed on the inside by the word of God so that His people would trust him despite our current circumstances, trials, or tribulations. This world has many illnesses, but the greatest of these is a sickness of the heart to be hardened towards the one true God .... If we don't correctly believe in the right identity of Jesus who is God we will die in our sins. Jesus came into the world to save sinners, we have set our hope on Him."[9]

That's the theme Paul picks up in verses 21 and 22: "And you, who once were alienated and enemies in your mind by wicked works, yet now He has reconciled in the body of His flesh through death."

This sentence is like a flashback in a movie. It's as if Paul is saying, "Don't forget where you were and what you were before you were reconciled to God by Christ's death on the cross." (See Ephesians 2:11-13.)

Sin alienates and separates us from God. So severe is that separation that the death of God's Son is the only thing that can bring reconciliation. It's impossible to overstate the effect that sin has on mankind.

John Phillips told the story of Leonardo da Vinci's painting *The Last Supper*. The great artist sought a long time for a man to use as a model for the image of Christ. He finally found a young man named Pietro Bandinelli, who was singing in one of the choirs in Rome. Da Vinci hired him to sit for him, as he immortalized his face as the face of Jesus Christ.

"Years passed," said Phillips. "Much of the painting was finished, but still the artist lacked a suitable model whom he could paint as Judas Iscariot, someone whose features bore the indelible marks of sin. Finally, he found a beggar, a man of villainous countenance, exactly suited to portray the face of the traitor. He hired the man, who sat stolidly while the artist transferred his features to the face of Judas on the canvas."[10]

You guessed it. The man was Pietro Bandinelli. A lifetime of moral carelessness and tolerated evil had left its mark on the man. All that lay between the man with the face of Jesus and the man with the face of Judas was a few short years of sin.

Sin debases character and ruins lives. Sin makes us enemies and aliens from God. But Christ's substitutionary death on the cross, which paid the full penalty for our sin, made it possible for us to be reconciled to God and at peace with Him eternally.

Reconciliation means we're no longer in a state of hostility with someone. When a man is reconciled with his wife or a teenager with her parents or a person with an estranged friend, the war is over. The relationship is restored, and peace reigns. When we live confidently in Christ, we have peace within because we have peace with God.

During World War II, Hiroo Onoda was a lieutenant in the Japanese army. In 1944, he was sent to the island of Lubang off the coast of the Philippines in order to hamper enemy attacks on the island. Under no circumstances was he to surrender. Unfortunately, nobody told him when the war ended.

Eating rice, coconuts, and meat from stolen cattle, Hiroo Onoda hid in the jungle for 29 years, carrying out occasional guerrilla activities and awaiting further instructions.

He avoided search parties sent to find him, believing they were enemy scouts. He didn't trust leaflets announcing the end of the war, assuming them to be propaganda. Newspapers, letters and family pictures dropped from the air were taken to be a trick. Friends and relatives even spoke out over loudspeakers, but Onoda remained suspicious. He didn't believe that the war had really ended.

Eventually, his former commanding officer was located, working as a bookseller in southern Japan. He flew to Lubang Island to officially read the terms of the cease-fire to Onoda and relieve him of duty. On March 9, 1974, nearly thirty years after the war had ended, Onoda finally surrendered.

Onoda was 22-years-old when left on the island. He returned a prematurely aged man of 52, saying, "Nothing pleasant happened in the 29 years in the jungle."[11]

How sad it is to be free and not know it! How much sadder it is to be free and to know it and to live like you don't know it!

We should be saying: "Redeemed! How I love to proclaim it!"

He Will Restore You (Jesus and Your Future)

The passage continues with these incredible words: "To present you holy, and blameless, and above reproach in His sight" (Colossians 1:22).

Paul reminded the Colossians the ultimate goal of Jesus Christ was not their personal salvation from their sin. The goal of Jesus Christ for them and for us is that one day Christ will be able to present us to the Father, "holy, and blameless, and above reproach in His sight."

In her book *Unashamed*, Heather Nelson writes, "The Christian's ultimate hope . . . is that we will be clothed in the honor of Jesus Christ when we stand before God in all his glory . . . . Imagine standing before God unashamed, with nothing to fear because both guilt and shame are gone forever. No more wounds in need of healing; no memories of past sin to cause you to turn away from our God of light and his people; nothing at all to darken this kingdom where God is the one illuminating each corner of his new creation. It will be like emerging from a grim black-and-white film to a vivid and bright happy ending—an ending without end, that stretches into forever."[12]

Those of us who know Christ are so forgiven our lives look to God like blindingly white snow (Isaiah 1:18). Yet we're prone to look back and dredge up our mistakes, and none of us get through even a single day without a slip-up somewhere. Oh, how wonderful to be saved one day—not just from the penalty and power—but from the very presence of sin!

He Is Remaking You (Jesus and Your Present)

One day we'll be perfect in our condition as well as in our position. Until then, God is working in our lives every day to bring us to maturity. The passage in Colossians goes on to tell us to "continue in the faith, grounded and steadfast . . . not moved away from the hope of the gospel which you heard, which was preached to every creature under heaven, of which I, Paul, became a minister" (Colossians 1:23).

When we receive Jesus Christ as Savior, it's not the ending of the process—it's the beginning. Jesus compared it to being born again, and we all know babies need to grow. Every day, our Lord is working in our lives to make us more like Himself. His desire is our discipleship; His goal is our godliness.

The Colossians letter challenges us to continue serving the One who redeemed us by His death on the cross. I like what Kent Hughes said about these verses: "The positive application of Paul's words is this: The Gospel does not work like magic. The mind, the heart, and the will must be involved. Our minds must feed on Christ and His Word. Our hearts are to focus on Him in love. Our wills are to take their practice and pattern from Him. Present faith leads to present results ... we must fill our lives every day from Him."[13]

The Gnostics had created a disruptive moment for the Colossian church. In some ways the recent pandemic has created a similar disruptive moment for us. As we seek to find our way in these uncertain times, Paul's words to the Colossians are good words for us as well: "Continue in the faith, grounded and steadfast, and ... not moved away from the hope of the gospel" (Colossians 1:23).

The word "grounded" means we are to lay a solid foundation for our faith. (See Ephesians 3:17.)

The word "steadfast" means we are to remain settled and constant on that foundation. If we do these two things, we'll be in no danger of moving away from the hope of the Gospel.

We need to keep ourselves at the foot of the cross, always remembering the eternal work Jesus wrought during His six hours of suffering.

As I was writing this book, an item appeared in the news about an oil painting by Sandro Botticelli. It was a portrait of Jesus Christ with bloodshot eyes and a halo made of tiny weeping angels. The name of the picture: *The Man of Sorrows*. It dates from around the year 1500, and it was sold at a Sotheby's auction in New York City for $45.4 million.

The expert at Sotheby's who studied the painting was a man named Christopher Apostle. According to a report on *Fox Business*, Mr. Apostle said infrared tests on the painting revealed that Botticelli started painting Christ as an infant, but at some point turned the canvas upside down and started over, painting Him as a man suffering during His passion.

I don't want you to miss the irony of this story. Mr. Apostle reviewed the life of Christ from birth to death, and it was worth over $45 million![14]

When in my hands I hold the apostle Paul's portrait of Christ in Colossians 1, explaining who He is and what He has done, I have a priceless treasure. It's just a few words, a handful of verses. But its value to you and me is inestimable. No painting can do Him justice. No auction can value His worth. No mind can conceive His greatness.

This is the fullness of Christ, who means all the world to you and me!

CHAPTER 4

Authentic Christian Ministry

COLOSSIANS 1:24 – 2:7

CAN A LIGHTHOUSE DO MORE HARM THAN GOOD? YES, IF it's not sitting in the right place.

A few hours south of Sydney, Australia, a lighthouse rose from the cliffs of Jervis Bay. It was badly needed along this dangerous coastline as ships arrived home from the Tasman Sea. The proposal came in 1856, and construction began in 1860. Imagine the alarm of the Pilots Board when it learned the actual building site was five miles from the proposed location. The map used to select the site had been incorrectly drawn.

When the lighthouse was finished on October 1, 1860, its beacon light couldn't be seen by ships approaching the harbor from the north, and it could barely be seen by vessels coming from the south. Nevertheless, the lighthouse remained until 1893, and it's blamed for 23 shipwrecks.

For more than thirty years, the lighthouse along the cliffs misled captain after captain and caused one shipwreck after another.[1]

That's what happens when we follow an uncertain light and are deceived by a false signal.

The apostle Paul was always concerned about shifting theological ground. When it came to spiritual truth, there was no room for error. When Gospel truth is misplaced or replaced, it causes personal wreckage. That's why Paul wrote to the Christians in the city of Colossae when he learned of false teachers in their area.

The false teachers who had infiltrated the church in Colossae had one big advantage over the apostle Paul. They were in Colossae while Paul was under arrest in Rome. They could command the Colossian believers' attention. They persuaded them with polished speeches and promises of a higher level of spiritual knowledge. They sowed seeds of doubt and confusion without being challenged by a formidable opponent. Their teaching of a substandard christ was creating a false Christian experience, as it always does.

That's why Paul wrote such a personal and pointed letter. He aimed to keep the Colossians and all the rest of us from falling prey to the false teaching that creeps into our environments. By pen, Paul wanted to do for them—and us—what he could not do in person: to equip them to recognize and reject any false teaching that can make a shipwreck of their faith.

That's why Paul opened with so much theological dynamite, as we've already seen. He held aloft the supremacy of Christ and the power of salvation.

Now, beginning in Colossians 1:24, Paul brought himself into the equation. He wanted the Colossians to realize he was an authentic minister of the authentic Gospel. I love this following paragraph because of its two great themes: the commitments and the concerns that anchor the hearts of those serving the true Christ. As a lifelong pastor, I've drawn courage from this passage, and I think you will too.

Let these words sink into your heart as we begin our study.

I now rejoice in my sufferings for you, and fill up in
my flesh what is lacking in the afflictions of Christ,
for the sake of His body, which is the church, of which
I became a minister according to the stewardship from
God which was given to me for you, to fulfill the word
of God, the mystery which has been hidden from ages
and from generations, but now has been revealed to
His saints. To them God willed to make known what
are the riches of the glory of this mystery among the
Gentiles: which is Christ in you, the hope of glory.
Him we preach, warning every man and teaching
every man in all wisdom, that we may present every
man perfect in Christ Jesus. To this end I also labor,
striving according to His working which works in me
mightily (Colossians 1:24-29).

The Commitments of Christian Ministry

As I said, there's a shift in verse 24, as Paul began speaking about himself as a preacher of the Gospel. Eight times in the next thirteen verses he refers to himself in the first person singular—I. We can put our own names there. While none of us are the apostle Paul, he's our model and mentor when it comes to personal ministry. If we take these verses personally, we'll be ready to serve the Lord as never before.

Get Ready to Suffer

Paul began verse 24 by saying, "I now rejoice in my sufferings for you, and fill up in my flesh what is lacking in the afflictions of Christ, for the sake of His body, which is the church."

Paul has sometimes been called the Job of the New Testament because of how much suffering he endured. One writer said, "Paul tells us that he was suffering. Even as he wrote this letter, he was chained to a jailer, having been falsely accused of assorted charges, some of them lethal. He could no longer travel and preach, and he could no longer evangelize great cities and plant new churches. His body was a mosaic of whip marks printed on his flesh by many a Hebrew lash and Roman scourge. Moreover he was chronically ill and in need of the constant care of a physician."[2]

Paul didn't rejoice in suffering for suffering's sake. He rejoiced because he was suffering "for the sake of . . . the church." All of the trouble he experienced in his ministry was worth it because the Church was expanding in Colossae and around the world.

When Paul spoke of filling up "what is lacking in the afflictions of Christ," he wasn't suggesting anything was missing in the suffering and death of Christ. That would invalidate what Jesus Himself said when the suffering was completed. He shouted from the cross, "It is finished!" (John 19:30)

When it comes to Christ's work on the cross, there's nothing more to be done. Nothing was left undone! Jesus paid it all!

What, then, did Paul mean by filling up in his own flesh "what is still lacking in regard to Christ's afflictions" (Colossians 1:24, NIV)?

In his study of Colossians, Kent Hughes wrote,

> Paul did not help with the atonement; that was
> Christ's solo work. But one thing that the phrase
> does teach for sure (and everyone agrees on this) is
> that a close identification develops between Christ
> and the Church through suffering. Before Paul's
> Damascus Road encounter, Paul had been making
> Christ suffer in the people he was persecuting. Christ's
> first words to Paul made this clear: "Saul, Saul, why
> are you persecuting Me?" (Acts 9:4). Jesus was being
> persecuted in the bodies of His followers. However,
> immediately after Paul's conversion Jesus said, "I will
> show him how much he must suffer for the sake of
> my name" (9:16). Now Paul would suffer, and Christ
> would suffer in him—a stupendous truth![3]

It's been nearly two thousand years since Paul wrote Colossians, but Christians are still suffering—in some places now more than ever. Even as I wrote this chapter, a story showed up in the news of Pastor Bashir Sengendo of Uganda. Once he was a Muslim mosque leader in the eastern part of his nation. He came to Christ on May 13, 2016, and soon thereafter attended Bible college for six months. He became a pastor.

His Muslim relatives begged him to return home to deal with a portion of property supposedly allocated to him. When Pastor Sengendo returned to his family's home in western Uganda, he was ambushed. His brother and uncle attacked him with a sharp weapon, wounding him in his head, back, and hand. His screams brought the police, and he was rushed to a local hospital. He died from the loss of blood, leaving behind a wife and four children—ages 10, 8, 5, and 2.

Most global news services don't carry many articles about Christian persecution, but if you look for them, you'll find tragedies like this occurring all over the world every single day.

As one pastor said, "Paul's sufferings fill up Christ's afflictions not by adding anything to their worth, but by extending them to the people they were meant to save .... God really means for the body of Christ, the church, to experience some of the suffering he experienced so that when we proclaim the cross as the way to life, people will see the marks of the cross in us and feel the love of the cross from us."[4]

Get Ready to Serve

Those who serve Christ share another commitment with Paul. They are ready to serve. The apostle wrote, "Of which I became a minister according to the stewardship from God which was given to me for you, to fulfill the word of God, the mystery which has been hidden from ages and from generations, but now has been revealed to His saints. To them God willed to make known what are the riches of the glory of this mystery among the Gentiles: which is Christ in you, the hope of glory" (Colossians 1:25-27).

Look at the word Paul used in verse 25: "minister." The Greek word he used is the same word from which we get our word *deacon*. The word simply means "a servant." It describes someone who serves. In that sense, all who know Christ are ministers.

Paul saw himself as a steward of God who was responsible to serve the Church by proclaiming a particular message. He referred to his message as a "mystery." Let's look at that word. The term "mystery" is found 22 times in the New Testament, the majority of those times in the writings of Paul.

When he used the word "mystery" in verse 26, he was not referring to the kind of mystery we think of in detective books. In biblical language, a mystery is a truth that cannot be discovered by human reasoning but only by divine revelation. It's something that has been hidden in the past but is now revealed to those who receive it by faith.

The mystery Paul was talking about here is the biblical revelation of the nature of the Church. The wall between Jews and Gentiles is gone, and the Lord's Church is one unified Body made up of those from every background who have declared Christ as Lord. Gentile believers are joined with Jews in one spiritual body, the Church, and they enjoy perfect equality, knowing the riches of the glory and hope that is found in Christ.

From both the Jewish and Gentile perspective, this seemed impossible because of the mutual disdain between Gentiles and Jews. This was indeed some kind of mystery!

"Bishop John Green of Sydney Australia tells about working with a group of boys, some aboriginal blood and some of English descent, and how the racial tensions were such that they would not sit peaceably with each other on the bus. One day when things were out of hand, he stopped the bus, ordered them all out, and told them they were no longer black and white but green. He lined them up in alternate order and made each one say, 'I'm green' as he got back on the bus. They drove along quietly 'integrated,' until he heard a voice from the back of the bus say, 'Okay, light green on one side and dark green on the other!'"[5]

The ancient Jews and Gentiles were like that, but with less humor!

Paul was saying, we are no longer alienated as Jews and Gentiles. We are all "in Christ"—"Christ in you, the hope of glory." The Amplified Bible says, "Christ in and among you" (Colossians 1:27). Christ is in Jew and Gentile, and He is the hope of glory for them both.

Paul was ready to suffer and ready to serve this glorious cause.

Get Ready to Speak

He was also ready to speak. Colossians 1:28 continues: "Him we preach, warning every man and teaching every man in all wisdom, that we may present every man perfect in Christ Jesus."

I like the way J. B. Phillips translated this verse: "So, naturally, we proclaim Christ! We warn everyone we meet, and we teach everyone we can, all that we know about him."

We warn everyone we meet and teach everyone we can!

Thirty years ago, Paul Brown went on a mission trip to Romania, and he prayed for ten people to come to Christ during the trip. As it happened, more than ten people found Christ as Savior. One of them was a man named Eugen. This year Eugen made his first ever trip to America, and he took a ten-hour train trip from New York City to visit Paul, who lives in Virginia with his daughter, Cyndi Logsdon.

"We all cried," said Cyndi. "It was just a beautiful testimony of the grace of God. It was an extremely tender and sweet time, and so often in life we don't get to see these things." Eugen said, "I've waited 30 years just to say thank you for your investment in my life, and I wanted to thank you for your prayers."

Cyndi added, "In some ways it was not surprising, because my Dad shares the Gospel with people everywhere he goes, and he's been like that his entire life."[6]

What a way to live!

Warren Wiersbe said, "The false teachers exalted themselves and their great 'spiritual' attainments. They preached a system of teaching, but Paul preached a Person. The gnostics preached philosophy and the empty traditions of men (Col. 2:8), but Paul proclaimed Jesus Christ. The false teachers had lists of rules and regulations (Col. 2:16, 20–21), but Paul presented Christ. What a difference in ministries!"[7]

We must warn everyone we meet and teach everyone we can!

Paul warned the lost about the coming judgment of God, and he warned the saved about drifting from their commitment to Christ and His truth. I enjoy teaching people more than warning them, but both are necessary. Think of the lighthouse I described earlier. Properly located, it would both warn the ship's crew and instruct them about the safest passage.

Paul uses the term "every" three times in this one verse. He reminds us of his strategy and of what our strategy should be: to evangelize every person, to edify every person, and to present every person complete in spiritual maturity in Christ.

That's our job—to evangelize, to edify, and to help people grow to maturity in Christ.

I read these words from one Bible teacher: "The false teachers ... had much to say about a wisdom for a peculiar few only (2:8, 18), but St. Paul's soul spurned such restrictions and rejoiced in a gospel for all .... A gospel for all people everywhere ... It is a message for rich and poor, old and young, respectable and outcast, peer and peasant."[8]

Get Ready to Struggle

Serving Christ also involves struggling—working hard and endeavoring to do our best. Paul continued, "To this end I also labor, striving according to His working which works in me mightily" (Colossians 1:29).

The Greek word translated "labor" was used for work which left one so weary it was as if a person had taken a beating. It denotes labor to exhaustion. The word "striving" is an even stronger term than labor. It's the Greek word from which we get our English word *agony*, and it was used for agonizing in an athletic event or in a fight. It implies a struggle.

Take these two words together—*labor* and *striving*—and you can see the tremendous energy of Paul's ministry. He strained every physical and moral muscle to present every man complete in Christ. Paul used some of these same words in describing his work ethic to Timothy: "For to this end we both labor and suffer reproach" (1 Timothy 4:10).

He mentioned something similar to the Thessalonian believers: "For you remember, brethren, our labor and toil; for laboring night and day, that we might not be a burden to any of you, we preached to you the gospel of God" (1 Thessalonians 2:9).

Nathaniel Pidgeon was a city evangelist in Australia, whose unusual ministry and exploits were recorded in his autobiography. He described one particular day full of open-air meetings and counseling. When evening came, he said, "I lay down very tired, which I mostly do after such a day. The conducting of those meetings falls my lot; giving out the hymns; speaking and praying all day together, with the anxiety of mind [that] lays the poor body prostrate. I lay down, as I had often done before, with a tired body and a happy soul—tired in the work, but not of it."

This is the frequent saying of those who are laboring for their Lord. They become tired in the work but not of it.

We're living in a day characterized by shorter work weeks, more breaks, lots of entertainment, abundant vacation sites, mindless video pursuits, and multiple retirement options. I'm not in favor of running ourselves into the ground or living in constant fatigue. But neither do I advocate a soft and easy Christian experience that only serves the Lord when it's convenient and pleasant.

Among the ranks of Christians there are both workers and shirkers. It's not hard to see which group Paul joined. He said about himself in another place: "I labored more abundantly than they all, yet not I, but the grace of God which was with me" (1 Corinthians 15:10).

Through the years, I confess I've sometimes felt like evangelist D. L. Moody, who was so exhausted one evening that his evening prayer was simply: "Lord, I'm tired. Amen!"[9]

I try not to end every day like that, but we only have so much time allocated for us on earth, and whatever we do for the Lord we're to work at it with all our heart.

This is the dynamic balance in the ministry of Christ: We work and Christ works. If we just wait for Christ to work, nothing gets done. If we work but don't wait for Christ to work, whatever gets done may not be Christ's desire for us. We'll certainly wear ourselves out trying to accomplish anything for Him in the energy of the flesh.

The Living Bible translates Colossians 1:29 like this: "This is my work, and I can do it only because Christ's mighty energy is at work within me." When that's true, we may grow fatigued. But we'll not burn out. We may grow weary in the work, but not of the work.

These, then, are the commitments Paul made to his ministry, and the Lord inspired him to record them so we, too, will be encouraged to get ready to suffer, to serve, to speak, and to struggle, striving with all our heart in the work of the Kingdom.

The Concerns of Christian Ministry

This ongoing commitment naturally led to a deep concern for the good of the people he was leading, and that's what we see in the opening verses of Colossians 2:

> For I want you to know what a great conflict I have for you and for those in Laodicea, and for as many as have not seen my face in the flesh, that their hearts may be encouraged, being knit together in love, and attaining to all riches of the full assurance of understanding, to the knowledge of the mystery of God, both of the Father and of Christ, in whom are hidden all the treasures of wisdom and knowledge (verses 1-3).

Paul was concerned for the Colossians to be courageous in heart, cooperative in love, confident in salvation, convinced of the truth, and consistent in the faith.

Courageous in Heart

Let's begin with developing a courageous heart. Verses 1 and 2 say: "For I want you to know what a great conflict I have for you and those in Laodicea, and for as many as have not seen my face in the flesh, that their hearts may be encouraged."

The reason Paul was suffering, struggling, and striving was for his readers—that their hearts may be encouraged. And remember, you are now his reader! These words are for you. During his lifetime, Paul suffered, persevered, and labored so that today, generations later, your heart can be encouraged.

In English, we often equate *heart* with emotions. But, in the Bible, *heart* refers to "the center of the personality, the source of willing and thinking in addition to feeling …. 'Encouragement in heart' … is therefore a way of referring to an encouragement that touches the deepest part of our being and that affects every aspect of our persons."[10]

In other words, your heart is YOU!

The term for "encouragement" is the Greek word *parakalein*. Sometimes that word meant "to comfort," sometimes "to exhort;" but always behind it is the idea of enabling a person to meet some difficult situation bravely and with confidence. A Greek historian used this word to describe how a general rallied his troops, who had lost heart in the battle and were dejected. As a result of his words, courage was reborn and a body of dispirited men became fit again for heroic action. That is what *parakalein* means here. Paul's concern is that the church be filled with the type of courage that can cope with any situation.[11]

The town of Inkberrow, Worcestershire, is said to be the darkest village in England, without a single streetlight. Its two thousand residents walk down inky dark streets at night. But some years ago, Christopher and Avril Rowlands bought a small fir tree costing six pounds. They used it as their first Christmas tree, then planted it in the front yard. They were taller than it was. But it grew! Today the tree towers over the village, and the Rowlands pack it with lights every Christmas. Since they live in the middle of the village, the whole town reflects the glow of the tree, which fills the village with joy, cheer, and light.

The headline in the news said: "Elderly Couple Living in UK's Darkest Village Lights Up the Sky."[12] Imagine the euphoria and joy that brightly-lit tree brought to the homes and hearts of the people of Inkberrow.

The Bible tells us to light up the sky. Whatever our age, we can pump encouragement into the hearts of others.

Cooperative in Love

The next phrase says, "Being knit together in love" (Colossians 2:2).

Paul wanted the Colossians to be courageous toward the circumstances of life and loving toward one another. He wanted them to cooperate with each another and remain pleasant and close in their relationships.

It's the picture of the parts of a human body being held together by ligaments to make it strong. The parts represent individual Christians, and the ligaments represent love. Love is what unites the different people in the Body of Christ, and it's a beautiful thing.

One of the great passages in the Bible on unity is from the Old Testament: "How wonderful and pleasant it is when brothers live together in harmony! For harmony is as precious as the anointing oil that was poured over Aaron's head, that ran down his beard and onto the border of his robe. Harmony is as refreshing as the dew from Mount Hermon that falls on the mountains of Zion. And there the Lord has pronounced his blessing, even life everlasting" (Psalm 133:1-3, NLT).

None of our churches are perfect, and no pastor on earth can do everything right all the time. No staff can serve without some differences of opinion arising here and there. But the writer of Psalm 133 claimed that cooperation among believers is a precious thing and a refreshing thing.

Be concerned about unity in the Church. Be a peacemaker, not a troublemaker!

John Phillips said, "We cannot unravel our lives from those of other believers. We come from different social backgrounds. We have different levels of education. Often we have been raised in different countries and cultures. But we are knit together .... A woman like Mary Magdalene is made one with a woman like Mary, the mother of Jesus. A man like Simon the Zealot is made one with Matthew the publican. Peter the doer is made one with John the dreamer. We share a common bond."[13]

Confident in Salvation

Paul goes on to yearn for his readers to be confident in their salvation. He said in Colossians 2:2-3: "And attaining to all riches of the full assurance of understanding, to the knowledge of the mystery of God, both of the Father and of Christ, in whom are hidden all the treasures of wisdom and knowledge."

Notice those two words: "full assurance"!

The false teachers in Colossae claimed that wisdom or understanding was hidden away in some type of mystical experience or higher knowledge. But Paul insisted that "all the treasures of wisdom and knowledge" are hidden in Christ. Jesus has all the information needed for us to have assurance!

- He said to the thief on the cross, "Assuredly, I say to you, today you will be with Me in Paradise" (Luke 23:43).

- He proclaimed in John's Gospel: "Most assuredly, I say to you, he who hears My word and believes in Him who sent Me has everlasting life, and shall not come into judgment, but has passed from death into life" (John 5:24).

- He said, "Most assuredly, I say to you, he who believes in Me has everlasting life" (John 6:47).

Steven J. Lawson put it this way: "God wants us to have a 'know-so' salvation. Figuratively speaking, He does not want you to be a question mark, all bent over in doubt with your head hung low. Rather, He wants you to be an exclamation mark, standing erect with head held high, strengthened by a God-produced confidence in your faith in Him."[14]

Sean Michel is a musician from "the swamps of New Orleans, Louisiana," as he puts it, who was on the sixth season of *American Idol*. His dad was a devoted atheist, and his mom was a practicing Christian. When he was thirteen, he made a commitment to Christ after reading a Gospel tract. He became serious about Bible study and being a part of church, and in college he studied theology and biblical exegesis. All the time, he was working on his music and writing songs. He also sang and played on mission trips. In 2006, Sean auditioned for *American Idol*, and he used the opportunity to share his faith.

During all this time, however, Sean struggled with having assurance of his salvation. Somewhere deep within him was a nagging fear he wasn't truly saved, that he wasn't actually a child of God. But one day he simply accepted God's promise that his salvation was secure, and he nailed it down by writing a song called "I Know I've Been Converted."

He said, "'I Know I've Been Converted' is a real declaration for me. I've always struggled with assurance of my salvation. Recording that song was a statement I felt like I had to make that I truly know that God has saved me and is changing me."[15]

It's one thing to be saved and another to truly know that God has saved you and is changing you. Paul didn't just want us to have assurance. He wanted us to have full assurance.

Convinced of the Truth

Full assurance comes as we are convinced of the truth, and so Paul continued by writing: "Now this I say lest anyone should deceive you with persuasive words" (Colossians 2:4).

Paul didn't say the Colossians have already been deceived, but he knew from experience that it was possible. He was afraid some of his readers would be led astray by the sheer eloquence of the false teachers. One New Testament scholar wrote: "A work of grace is followed by an attack from the enemy, and ... one regular form this attack may take is the clever plausibility of teaching near enough to the truth to be apparently respectable and far enough away from it to be devastating in its effect on individuals and congregations."[16]

When Billy Graham was a young preacher, he began having doubts about the truthfulness of Scripture. He attended a Bible conference at Forest Home in California, and he overheard that someone had said something like, "Poor Billy .... He'll be circumscribed to a small little narrow interpretation of the Bible, and his ministry will be curtailed."

Deeply troubled, Billy went to his cabin and read again Bible passages about the authority of Scripture, and he noticed now Jesus loved the Scriptures and quoted them constantly. Leaving the cabin, Billy wandered into the forest, saying, "Lord, what shall I do?"

"So I went back and I got my Bible, and I went out in the moonlight. And I got to a stump and put the Bible on the stump, and I knelt down, and I said, 'Oh, God; I cannot prove certain things, I cannot answer some of the questions ... but I accept this Book by faith as the Word of God.'"

Shortly afterward at the 1949 Los Angeles Crusade, Billy Graham was catapulted to worldwide fame and to the beginning of a faithful ministry that lasted until his death at nearly one hundred years of age.[17]

It's hard to do much for the Lord when we're riddled with doubts about the integrity of Scripture. We must be convinced of the Truth—and the Truth sets us free to be greatly used by God.

Consistent in the Faith

Paul's final concern was that the Christians in Colossae remain steadfast in their faith, continuing to walk with Jesus. He went on to say: "For though I am absent in the flesh, yet I am with you in spirit, rejoicing to see your good order and the steadfastness of your faith in Christ. As you therefore have received Christ Jesus the Lord, so walk in Him, rooted and built up in Him and established in the faith, as you have been taught, abounding in it with thanksgiving" (Colossians 2:5-7).

Paul's command to "walk in Him" is the first imperative in the entire letter, and it sums up the message of the book in just three simple words.

Now, Paul ends our lesson with three different terms drawn from three different walks of life. Each is used to illustrate the nature of spiritual progress:

Rooted is an agricultural word. The tense of the Greek word means "once and for all having been rooted." Christians are not to be tumbleweeds that have no roots and are blown about by "every wind of doctrine" (Eph. 4:14). Nor are they to be "transplants" that are repeatedly moved from soil to soil. Once we are rooted by faith in Christ, there is no need to change the soil! The roots draw up the nourishment so that the tree can grow. The roots also give strength and stability ....

Built up is actually an architectural term. It is in the present tense: "being built up." When we trust Christ to save us, we are put on the foundation; from then on, we grow in grace ....

The word *abounding* was often used by Paul. It suggests the picture of a river overflowing its banks. Our first experience in the Lord is that of drinking the water of life by faith, and He puts within us an artesian well of living water (John 4:10-14). But that artesian well should become a "river of living water" (John 7:37-39) that grows deeper and deeper .... Our lives are shallow trickles instead of mighty rivers.[18]

I'm thankful for Paul's commitment and concern for the Colossians. But I'm even more thankful for Christ's commitment and concern for me! How Paul ministered to the Colossians is just a small picture of how Christ ministers to us. And when we stay rooted and established in Him, we will find ourselves serving others like He has served us: "Therefore if there is any consolation in Christ, if any comfort of love, if any fellowship of the Spirit, if any affection and mercy, fulfill my joy by being like-minded, having the same love, being of one accord, of one mind. Let nothing be done through selfish ambition or conceit, but in lowliness of mind let each esteem others better than himself. Let each of you look out not only for his own interests, but also for the interests of others" (Philippians 2:1-4).

CHAPTER 5

Beware

COLOSSIANS 2:8-23

RITA MCCLAIN'S SPIRITUAL JOURNEY BEGAN IN IOWA, where she grew up in a very narrow and peculiar church environment. In her twenties, she began attending a church that deemphasized doctrine, but she found one extreme as bad as the other. Within a few years, McClain had rejected all organized religion, claiming she had been wounded by Christianity because of her negative church experiences. For the next eighteen years, she sought inner peace in nature, through rock climbing in the mountains or hiking in the desert. That seemed enough for a while.

A few years later, in the aftermath of an emotionally draining divorce, McClain plunged into a series of religious experiences. Just as she had once explored mountains, she began scouting the inner landscape. She started with Unity, a metaphysical church near her California home. "It was a revelation, light-years away from the Old Testament kind of thing I knew very well from my childhood" she said.

"The next stop was Native American spiritual practices. Then it was Buddhism at Marin County's Spirit Rock Meditation Center, where she attended a number of retreats, including one that required eight days of silence.

"These disparate rituals melded into a personal religion," which McClain began celebrating at an altar in her home—an altar consisting "of an angel statue, a small bottle of 'sacred water' blessed at a women's vigil, a crystal ball, a pyramid, a small image of Buddha sitting on a brass leaf, a votive candle, a Hebrew prayer, a tiny Native American basket from the 1850s and a picture of her 'most sacred place,' a madrone tree near her home."[1]

If you can picture that, you can visualize what was starting to happen in the city of Colossae. The false teachers there were much like Rita. They borrowed from everything to create their doctrine, which evolved as it went along. The Colossian heresy seems to be a combination of rituals, restrictions, regulations, and mysticism. No wonder Paul was concerned when he learned some of this was starting to seep into the church.

This chapter deals with a long passage—Colossians 2:8-12—in which the apostle warned the Christians against five major errors of Gnosticism. According to John Phillips, those five errors can be labeled as: intellectualism (2:8-10), ritualism (2:11-13), legalism (2:14-17), mysticism (2:18-19), and asceticism (2:20-23).

It seems hard to believe, but after nearly two thousand years, these errors are still here—all of them!—to deceive and destroy those beguiled by them. Think of them as five ways of trading the abundant Christian life for a life marked by spiritual slavery and condemnation.

You've heard about the apparent decline in Christianity in America and the West, about plunging church attendance figures among young people, the rising percentage of those who are "nones" (with no identified religion), and the void created by rabid secularism. But I'm actually optimistic about the Lord's work. There's a younger generation growing up zealous for Jesus, and our Lord's Church is resilient. Nevertheless, we need to harbor in our hearts the same kind of concern for our churches and our children as we see in Paul's heart as he wrote to the Colossians.

He told them to "Beware," after which he listed his five areas of concern.

Intellectualism

He began with intellectualism. Now, few people have possessed the intellect of the apostle Paul. He was well-schooled, and he must have been a genius. He was not opposed to education or intellect itself. But remember, the word *gnostic* comes from the Greek word for *knowledge*, and the Gnostics boasted of their intellectualism. Simply put, they considered themselves smarter than everyone else. They felt their opinions were on a higher level.

They were, in fact, common thieves. Colossians 2:8 says, "Beware lest anyone cheat you through philosophy and empty deceit, according to the tradition of men, according to the basic principles of the world."

Someone wanted to rob the Colossians of their Christian faith and to cheat them out of the blessings of Christ through philosophy and empty deceit.

We might add the word *erroneous* before "philosophy." The word "philosophy" simply means "the love of wisdom." Paul was warning against a kind of philosophy that was being imported into the church in Colossae—a philosophy that was empty and deceitful and seduced believers away from the simplicity of their faith in Christ.

This same ideology is being imported into our culture and into our churches as well. One writer captured the erroneous philosophies of our times like this:

> God helps those who help themselves; He will love us more if we are good; He will judge us according to our accomplishments; Anything that feels good must be good; Self-expression is the only way to self-realization; Enjoyment is enrichment; Christ is the best of all good men—an example of living for us, nothing more; What we are is what we acquire; Our worth is determined by our productivity ....
>
> And so it goes—everything from playboy philosophy to materialism, astrology to scientism, sensualism to sorcery—is seeking to possess the American mind to manipulate our behavior and motivate our spending. And often Christians are among those who respond because their emptiness has not been filled with the fullness of Christ. His fullness fills our emptiness.[2]

The Four Marks of Intellectualism

There may be a million false philosophies and thousands of versions of intellectualism, but they all share some common traits—four of them, as Paul lays it out.

Intellectualism Is Deceptive

Colossians 2:8 says, "Beware lest anyone cheat you through philosophy and empty deceit." J. B. Phillips translates this phrase, "Through intellectualism or high-sounding nonsense."

The word *philosophy* is found nowhere else in the Bible. It's a reference to "the highest effort of the intellect." It is the best the human mind can do. But without God in the equation, Paul describes it as "empty deceit."

The key word here is *deceit*. This word occurs eighteen times in the New Testament, and it is most often used of Satan and his works. The devil is the original deceiver. False philosophies are deceptive because they all are very mysterious, complicated, and high-minded. Ignorant people can espouse them and babble on, sounding smart.

Dr. Donald Grey Barnhouse, the great preacher and writer, used to illustrate this by telling of a practical joke which he and his teenage friends played on some unsuspecting passersby in a large city.

His group stood on a busy street corner and stared intently into the air. One of them pointed, while another said (loudly enough to be overheard), "It is not." A third friend argued, "It is so!" At this, one or two people stopped and began to look up in the same direction as Barnhouse and his friends. As the argument grew more heated, others stopped to gaze fixedly at the point the group discussed. Then, one by one, Barnhouse and his friends quietly slipped out of the crowd and gathered a few yards away to watch the results.

By this time, some fifteen people were looking into the air. The crowd changed as new passersby came along and joined the group. Twenty minutes later several were still leaning against a building, looking up for something that wasn't there and never had been.

Barnhouse said, "That little incident is a good illustration of all the earth-born religions. People talk about having faith; they tell you to look in a direction where there is absolutely nothing. Some people are so desperately in need of seeing something that they will look till they are almost blind, yet they never catch a glimpse of anything real."[3]

Intellectualism Claims Antiquity

Intellectualism also claims antiquity. Paul continued, "Beware lest anyone cheat you through philosophy and empty deceit, *according to the tradition of men*" (Colossians 2:8, emphasis added).

All cults claim antiquity. They may have just recently been invented, but they say their new revelations are from ancient traditions. And in a way, they do all go back to the devil's ploy in the Garden of Eden. Jesus said to some of His critics, "You are of your father the devil .... When he speaks a lie, he speaks from his own resources, for he is a liar and the father of it" (John 8:44).

There are no new lies, just new versions of the old ones. In a recent *New York Times* bestseller, *Live Not By Lies*, Rod Dreher tells about receiving a phone call from an eminent American physician, whose elderly mother, "a Czechoslovak immigrant to the United States, had spent six years of her youth as a political prisoner in her homeland." She had been part of the resistance. "Now in her nineties and living with her son and his family," she observed that the events "in the United States today reminded her of when communism first came to Czechoslovakia." She was referring to cancel culture and the growing discrimination against Christians.[4]

Today's lies have tendrils in their roots that extend back to the serpent in Eden. Intellectualism has no problem claiming antiquity—the traditions of men.

Intellectualism Is Demonic

That brings us to the next phrase in Colossians 2:8: "Beware lest anyone cheat you through philosophy and empty deceit ... *according to the basic principles of the world*" (emphasis added). The two words *basic principles*, are better translated "elemental spirits." This expression usually invokes Satanic forces. The New International Version says, "See to it that no one takes you captive through hollow and deceptive philosophy, which depends on human tradition *and the elemental spiritual forces of this world*" (emphasis added).

I believe Paul was arguing that unseen evil forces were in control of the false doctrine that was corrupting the Colossians, and there were demons trying to bring the Colossians back to the bondage they had known before they were saved.

I just spent the better part of a year researching the philosophy of socialism, and I can tell you it is demon controlled. Its founder, Karl Marx, was possessed by a demon and his doctrine is a devil's doctrine. First John 5:19 says, "We know that we are children of God, and that the whole world is under the control of the evil one" (NIV).

The whole world is under the control of Satan—except for those of us who are children of God in this world through Jesus Christ. The philosophies that drive our educational system, infiltrate our politics, dilute our theology, pervade our media, and divide our world—they are all spun from the web of the enemy.

Intellectualism Is Enslaving

No wonder intellectualism is enslaving. Listen to Colossians 2:8 in the New Living Translation: "Don't let anyone capture you with empty philosophies and high-sounding nonsense that come from human thinking and from the spiritual powers of this world, rather than from Christ."

This is one of three imperative warnings that Paul presents in these verses. That opening phrase about being captured means: "to take someone captive and to carry them off as if they were a prisoner of war."

People who get caught up in false doctrine and heresy don't often recover and come back to the Lord. Cults hopelessly enslave people.[5] If you're dabbling in strange doctrine or listening to arrogant teaching that doesn't ring true, my advice to you is to run as fast as you can away from such seductive philosophy. Get out while you can get out! Get out before it is too late! Renounce anything that does not see Christ as everything!

The *Tampa Bay Times* ran a story about a woman named Evelyn, who met a wonderful man through an online dating service. Robert Wilson was 62, fit, and well-off. Evelyn had moved to Florida after a long career with a technology company. The two talked on the phone and texted daily, and they decided to get married in the Bahamas. What she didn't know was that Wilson was part of a team of organized criminals who were running romance scams based out of Nigeria. By the time Evelyn learned the awful truth, her bank accounts were gone, her retirement account was drained, and she had to get a job at a local store to buy her next meal. "I lost everything," she said. "I'll be dealing with this the rest of my life."

She's not alone. Floridians are losing millions of dollars every month to romance scams, with the average victim losing thousands of dollars. Advocates for the victims say, "A critical thing to know is that virtually everyone can be scammed. It's only a question of the right grooming and right story."[6]

It's one thing to lose your financial freedom. It's even worse to be scammed by false teachers who want to destroy your spiritual freedom and eternal hopes.

The Folly of Abandoning Christ

The last part of verse 8 describes the folly of following any philosophy that isn't centered on an accurate view of Christ: "Don't let anyone capture you with empty philosophies and high-sounding nonsense that come from human thinking and from the spiritual powers of this world, *rather than from Christ*" (NLT, emphasis added).

When you keep your eyes on Jesus, knowing Him by faith and fellowshiping with Him in Scripture, when you walk with Him and talk with Him, when you are close to Him, it's very hard for the lies of intellectualism to overtake you.

That brings Paul back to his great emphasis—the Lord Jesus Christ in all His supremacy. The next two verses say, "For in Him dwells all the fullness of the Godhead bodily; and you are complete in Him, who is the head of all principality and power" (Colossians 2:9-10).

The Gnostics were trying to say the fullness of God was spread out and divided among angels and various spiritual agencies. Paul responded by declaring that the fullness of God dwells only in Jesus Christ. The Godhead has taken up permanent residence in the body of Jesus.

John Philips wrote: "The body of Jesus was fashioned by the Holy Spirit in the virgin's womb. In that body, Jesus lived and displayed His essential deity. In that body, He died. In that same body, He rose from the dead. In that body, He ascended into heaven. And in that body, He is now seated on the throne of God, serving as our great High Priest. In that body, He is to come again to sit upon the throne of David and rule over the empires of earth. That body is now His forevermore."[7]

In Jesus Christ is the Godhead, the essence of deity.

Paul later wrote a similar thought to Timothy: "And without controversy great is the mystery of godliness: God was manifested in the flesh" (1 Timothy 3:16).

Christ is God in a body. And since Christ is in us (Colossians 1:27), we can understand Paul's statement to the

Colossians: "And you are complete in Him, who is the head of all principality and power" (Colossians 2:10).

Here is the wonder of this statement: God is in Christ, and Christ is in us. Our fullness comes from His fullness. That doesn't mean we become God Himself, of course. Only God is God, and living a godly life doesn't turn us into little gods. But through His precious promises we can become more like Him. We can possess His joy, His patience, His wisdom, His influence, and His priorities.

When we have Christ in us, we are so mystically united to Him, that, as members of His body, we share His life to the fullest. That's the most protected place to be.

Ritualism

As we come to the next verse, Colossians 2:11, we're confronted with another danger—ritualism. The Colossian heresy had various elements, and Paul alludes to another by writing: "In Him you were also circumcised with the circumcision made without hands, by putting off the body of the sins of the flesh, by the circumcision of Christ" (Colossians 2:11).

As I've studied the book of Colossians, it's become evident to me that elements of the false doctrine invading the church had some kind of Jewish roots to them. The false teachers in Colossae were trying to bring their old Judaism into their new Christianity. Part of the Gnostic cocktail of doctrines was the requirement that believers in Christ be circumcised to be saved.

Many of the converts of the Early Church were Jewish converts. They'd grown up with a lifetime of rituals and ceremonies. When they accepted Christ, they struggled to leave behind the now unnecessary elements of their Jewish way of life. They were conflicted by the freedom of grace in light of all the ceremonies and feasts and dietary restrictions they had embraced as Jews. This tension is seen throughout the book of Acts (especially in chapter 15), as well as in books like Galatians and Hebrews.

The Ritual

One of the most stubborn battles involved the ceremony of circumcision. It's an indelicate subject to discuss for us today, but for the Jews it was central to their religion and orthodoxy. Circumcision was a minor surgical operation that involved the removal of a small portion of flesh from an infant Jewish boy when he was eight days old.

This Jewish ceremony was instituted by God as a sign and seal of the Abrahamic covenant. It was solely a Jewish custom, but Paul used this Old Testament Jewish ceremony to help the Colossians understand that our "circumcision" as Christians is much more extensive than the Jewish custom that predated it.

Our circumcision as Christians is a spiritual one—"the circumcision … of the heart," as Paul said in Romans 2:29. At salvation, believers undergo a spiritual surgery by "putting off the body of the sins of the flesh" (Colossians 2:11). This is the new birth, the new creation in conversion.

The Gnostics wanted to force the Colossian believers to undergo Old Testament physical circumcision as a requirement for salvation and spiritual enlightenment. Paul was refuting this with every ounce of mental and spiritual strength available to him through the power of Christ. If anything is added to the faith requirement of salvation, that addition, whatever it is, negates the whole issue of conversion.

The Reality

In an interesting turn of symbols, Paul brought up the subject of baptism. Look at verses 11 and 12 again: "In Him you were also circumcised with the circumcision made without hands, by putting off the body of the sins of the flesh, by the circumcision of Christ, *buried with Him in baptism, in which you also were raised with Him through faith in the working of God, who raised Him from the dead*" (Colossians 2:11-12, emphasis added).

The outward affirmation of the already accomplished inner transformation is now the believer's baptism by water. Christian baptism by immersion pictures the relationship with Jesus Christ in His death, burial, and resurrection. The act of baptism represents our identification with the death, burial, and resurrection of Christ.

The result of our identification with and allegiance to Christ is given in the next verse: "And you, being dead in your trespasses and the uncircumcision of your flesh, He has made alive together with Him, having forgiven you all trespasses" (Colossians 2:13).

Almost every Sunday at our church in California, we have the joy of witnessing men, women, boys, and girls being baptized. Each one takes a moment to read or share the story of how they came to Christ and what He has done for them. The stories could fill a book. Each is miraculous and glorious. It's not the ritual of baptism that changes them, and ritualism itself isn't where the power lies. The power is in the saving force of the cross of Jesus Christ.

Legalism

Closely connected to ritualism is legalism, and this is the next subject Paul broaches. He wrote, "Having wiped out the handwriting of requirements that was against us, which was contrary to us. And He has taken it out of the way, having nailed it to the cross. Having disarmed principalities and powers, He made a public spectacle of them, triumphing over them in it" (Colossians 2:14-15).

In ancient times, when someone needed to borrow money or anything else, a list was made and the person signed it. It was a debt. According to Paul, our debt before God was immeasurable. Our failure to obey God and our sinful behavior are like IOUs that are owed to God. But the Lord Jesus took those decrees that were against us, and He nailed them to the cross and forgave us everything.

In one of my favorite paraphrases of the New Testament, J. B. Phillips renders this verse like this: "He has forgiven you all your sins: Christ has utterly wiped out the damning evidence of broken laws and commandments which hung always over our heads, and has completely annulled it by nailing it over his own head on the cross" (Colossians 2:14).

Kent Hughes wrote,

Martin Luther experienced the reality of this truth in a dream in which he was visited at night by Satan, who brought to him a record of his own life, written with his own hand. The tempter said to him, "Is that true, did you write it?" The poor terrified Luther had to confess it was all true. Scroll after scroll was unrolled, and the same confession was wrung from him again and again and again. At length the Evil One prepared to take his departure, having brought Luther down to the lowest depths of abject misery. Suddenly the Reformer turned to the Tempter and said: "It is true, every word of it, but write across it all: 'The blood of Jesus Christ, God's Son, cleanses us from all sins.'"[8]

A great old hymn says,

> I need no other argument,
> I need no other plea
> It is enough that Jesus died,
> and that He died for me!

Colossians 2:16-17 goes on to say, "So let no one judge you in food or in drink, or regarding a festival or a new moon or sabbaths, which are a shadow of things to come, but the substance is of Christ."

Notice the legalism Paul is fighting here. He warns against two distinct categories of legalistic living, one involving diets and the other involving days.

Apparently there were those among the false teachers in Colossae who were trying to reinstitute the dietary rules of the Old Testament law as a means of enhancing one's spiritual life.

I read recently about a young man who suffered from a crippling form of arthritis. After he became a Christian, he met a doctor who put him on this "incredible" diet. The basic philosophy behind the diet was simple—never mix proteins and carbohydrates in the same meal. The young man swore that he had been healed completely by the diet. In the enthusiasm of his new faith and his new diet, he began to push for the incorporation of this new diet into the doctrinal statement of the church. Certainly God wants us all to be healthy, and what could be more health-giving than requiring that this God given diet be added?

One day when they were arguing about this issue in a church meeting, another young Christian spoke up and settled the issue once and for all.

"You believe that the Lord Jesus Christ is God, don't you?" he asked the one who was pushing the diet.

"Yes!"

"Would you also agree then that since the Lord Jesus Christ is our Creator, and the one who made our bodies, He would know what is best for those bodies, right?"

And again a resounding, "Right!"

"Then if your diet is right, why did the Lord Jesus feed loaves and fishes to five thousand people? He gave them proteins and carbohydrates at the same meal."

It's so much fun to know the Bible! The better we know God's Word, the more sense we have in evaluating the fads and quirks of our age.

Thankfully, we have a great deal of doctrinal teaching in the New Testament concerning dietary requirements. On one occasion when Jesus was eating something that the Pharisees considered unclean, He spoke to them in these words: "'Are you thus without understanding also? Do you not perceive that whatever enters a man from outside cannot defile him, because it does not enter his heart but his stomach, and is eliminated, thus purifying all foods?' And He said, 'What comes out of a man, that defiles a man'" (Mark 7:18-20).

Paul concluded this in his first letter to the Corinthians, saying, "But food does not commend us to God; for neither if we eat are we the better, nor if we do not eat are we the worse" (1 Corinthians 8:8).

Dietary discipline is not a sign of spirituality! Yes, we absolutely should maintain a healthy diet. We want to keep our bodies healthy for the Lord's service. But whether you eat a vegetable or a steak has no bearing on your eternal destiny. It's not your diet that saves you—it's your Deliverer, Jesus Christ.

The same is true regarding the observance of days! The Jews had their feast days and their Sabbath celebrations. When Jesus died and rose again on the third day, which was the first day of the week, everything changed.

Colossians 2:17 says the Old Testament patterns were shadows—they foreshadowed the Gospel. The Old Testament rituals and regulations were all pointing toward Christ. These things in themselves did not quantify spirituality. We are who we are because of Christ, not because of our observance of a set of regulations.

I grew up in a legalistic church atmosphere, and it almost made me want to run from the church and not toward it. When I finally discovered the principle of grace, it was like fresh wind blowing all around me. I did not become more tolerant of bad behavior. I became more careful because I didn't want to do anything to offend the One who had done so much for me!

When our spirituality is imposed from outside us, it leads to hypocrisy and legalism. When it is generated within us by the Holy Spirit, it leads to growing righteousness and abiding joy.

Max Anders has a lot to say about the evil of legalism: "Legalism—measuring your own or someone else's spirituality by the ability to keep manmade rules—is a rigid, confining, and lifeless way to live. It is easy because all it requires is a list of rules coupled with dutiful compliance. Wisdom or the skillful application of biblical principles to life's situations is unnecessary. Just comply. Legalism is not only rigid and lifeless, but it also fosters hypocritical pride. The Pharisees (ancient and modern) prove that. A focus on conformity to a code can cause one to forget things like arrogant pride, smug judgmentalism, anger, and a host of other dark sins that never seem to make the list."[9]

Mysticism

Having dealt with intellectualism, ritualism, and legalism, Paul turned his attention to mysticism. Colossians 2:18-19 says: "Let no one cheat you of your reward, taking delight in false humility and worship of angels, intruding into those things which he has not seen, vainly puffed up by his fleshly mind, and not holding fast to the Head, from whom all the body, nourished and knit together by joints and ligaments, grows with the increase that is from God."

The Colossians were not to allow anyone to distract them with false teaching that would keep them from true spiritual progress—progress that would bring its reward in Christ.

The Gnostic worship experience being pitched to the Colossians began with initiation into supposedly supernatural visions in which the individual was ushered into the heavenly realms to worship the angels. The worshiper would then return with all kinds of stories about what he had seen in his vision. The Colossians were being falsely told that if they really wanted to reach new levels of spirituality they needed to engage in these kinds of experiences. The mystical journey was intended to restore a lost dimension to spiritual experience.

"This quest for superspiritual experience ... fosters pride. The experience seeker delights in false humility, but his unspiritual mind puffs him up with idle notions. Believers may have spiritual experiences of varying kinds. Experiences themselves are not evil. When we try to make our experience the standard for all believers or when we measure our own or someone else's spirituality on the basis of that experience, we're being arrogant and unspiritual. Christ is central. Not rules. Not experiences."[10]

Vance Havner wrote, "Some people think they are Mystics when they are only Mistakes!"[11]

Asceticism

The final threat Paul attacked was asceticism. Look at Colossians 2:20-23: "Therefore, if you died with Christ from the basic principles of the world, why, as though living in the world, do you subject yourselves to regulations—'Do not touch, do not taste, do not handle,' which all concern things which perish with the using—according to the commandments and doctrines of men? These things indeed have an appearance of wisdom in self-imposed religion, false humility, and neglect of the body, but are of no value against the indulgence of the flesh."

Asceticism is the idea that self-denial is a way to earn favor from God. Asceticism is an entirely negative approach to life. It is characterized by the words *no* and *don't*. "Don't touch this. Make sure you don't taste this. You'd better not touch that."

In his commentary on Colossians, Max Anders wrote, "Asceticism ... teaches that depriving the body of its normal desires is a means of achieving greater holiness and approval from God .... It certainly looks spiritual when someone goes through all sorts of sacrifices supposedly to bring them closer to God. Asceticism has taken different shapes over time: wearing thick hair shirts close to the skin (as if itching is spiritual); sleeping on hard beds; whipping oneself; or prolonged fasting .... Paul says this kind of behavior has no value in restraining sensual indulgence."[12]

Dennis DeHaan related this story first told by Peter Kreeft:

A poor European family ... saved for years to buy tickets to sail to America. Once at sea, they carefully rationed the cheese and bread they had brought for the journey. After 3 days, the boy complained to his father, "I hate cheese sandwiches. If I don't eat anything else before we get to America, I'm going to die."

Giving the boy his last nickel, the father told him to go to the ship's galley and buy an ice-cream cone.

When the boy returned a long time later with a wide smile, his worried dad asked, "Where were you?"

"In the galley, eating three ice-cream cones and a steak dinner!"

"All that for a nickel?"

"Oh, no, the food is free," the boy replied. "It comes with the ticket."

DeHaan said, "The apostle Paul warned his readers about false teachers who were offering them 'bread and cheese' instead of 'steak.' They were in danger of forgetting Christ's sufficiency and relying on their own self-effort. We who have trusted Christ for salvation have been assured not only of safe passage to heaven but also of everything we need to live for Him here and now."[13]

So don't be intimidated by the spiritual bullies around you. You are complete and righteous in Christ! Remember the three warnings in this passage:

- "Beware lest anyone cheat you"—Colossians 2:8

- "Let no one judge you"—Colossians 2:16

- "Let no one cheat you"—Colossians 2:18

Recently a 73-year-old grandmother named Jean in Seaford, New York, received a phone call. A voice claiming to be her grandson said he had been arrested for drunk driving and was in jail. He begged her to help him. After several calls back and forth, a person claiming to be the grandson's lawyer told her he needed $8,000 for bail. Jean told him she had that much money in her home, and shortly afterward a man pretending to be a bail bondsman arrived to collect the cash. Jean handed him the envelope.

But the envelope was filled with worthless paper, and a police officer stepped out to arrest the imposter. Jean had sensed from the first moment that she was being tricked, and she wasn't about to fall for it. She called the police and played along only until they could make the arrest and stop the perpetrators.[14]

Good for her!

Let's fight back against the lies of the devil and the philosophies of this world. We have truth on our side and the Truth Himself in our hearts. Beware lest anyone cheat you. Let no one judge you. And let no one cheat you out of the blessings of the richness of Christ.

CHAPTER 6

What It Means to Be "In Christ"

COLOSSIANS 3:1-11

ON APRIL FOOL'S DAY, 2012, PHILADELPHIA CITY officials used tape to create an "E-Lane" on the sidewalk for pedestrians outside downtown office buildings. What's an E-Lane? It's a lane for pedestrians walking head-down while using their smartphone.

The goal was to get them into a corridor of their own to keep them from colliding with other pedestrians—and to keep them from falling off the curb, wandering into traffic, and running into light poles.

Most people didn't get the joke; they thought the E-Lane was a permanent addition. In fact, when the tape on the sidewalk was removed after April Fool's, city hall received some complaints from citizens who thought the smartphone lane was a great idea!

After Philadelphia security camera footage went viral on the Internet—showing a young man using his phone, falling off a deserted train station platform late at night, and lying stunned on the tracks for several minutes—officials decided a safety campaign was in order. (The young man recovered and scrambled to safety before the next train came along.)

Rina Cutler, a Philadelphia deputy mayor for transportation and public utilities, said, "One of the messages will certainly be 'Pick Your Head Up!'"[1]

What happened in Philadelphia parallels a rich biblical truth expressed in Colossians 3. We can learn a lesson from Rina Cutler—and from the apostle Paul—about the benefit of "picking our head up" and turning our attention to heavenly things.

As we come to Colossians 3, you'll notice a shift in tone and topic. The first two chapters of Colossians are filled with theological and doctrinal truths about Jesus Christ. Beginning in chapter 3, Paul draws out the implications of these truths for our daily lives. Out of doctrine comes duty. Out of biblical content comes godly character.

We often see this in Paul's writings. He knew there must be biblical content before there can be biblical conduct. Some Bible teachers are heavy on content, but give little practical application. Others devote most of their time to application, but they shortchange the doctrinal teachings that provide the foundation for our behavior.

Paul always had the right balance. In Colossians, he described our blessings in Christ, and now, beginning with chapter 3, he's going to describe our behavior in Christ. To put it another way, the first half of Colossians tell us how God has changed us, and the last half of Colossians is going to show us how He is still changing us.

Once again, the key to it all is Jesus Christ, who is mentioned four times in the first four verses of our text. This passage is short, but worthy of memorization, for every word is profound:

> If then you were raised with Christ, seek those things which are above, where Christ is, sitting at the right hand of God. Set your mind on things above, not on things on the earth. For you died, and your life is hidden with Christ in God. When Christ who is our life appears, then you also will appear with Him in glory (Colossians 3:1-4).

In Christ You Are a New Person

Prepositions are important words. The one we choose to use makes a difference in what we're saying. Try explaining to a five-year-old the difference between throwing the ball *to* his little brother or *at* his little brother!

In the passage above, you can circle the word "with" three times.

And speaking of grammar, notice how these three "withs" correspond to three different tenses—three time zones in our lives.

- "You were raised *with* Christ" (Colossians 3:1, emphasis added). That's the past tense.

- "Your life is hidden *with* Christ in God" (Colossians 3:3, emphasis added). This is in the present tense.

- "You also will appear *with* Him in glory" (Colossians 3:4, emphasis added). Here we have the future tense.

Before we look at those three phrases, let's notice one other word in this passage—"died." Right in the middle of the passage—in verse 3—we learn that we died. This is a point heard in very few sermons, but it's New Testament truth. When we receive Jesus Christ as our Savior, there is a sense in which we die.

Earlier in Colossians, Paul said, "You died with Christ from the basic principles of the world" (Colossians 2:20). Romans 6:8 says, "Now if we died with Christ, we believe that we shall also live with Him."

When Jesus died, we died with Him (Galatians 2:20). When He was buried, so were we (Romans 6:4). We also shared in His glorious resurrection (Colossians 3:1), so we can be seated in the heavenlies with Him (Ephesians 2:6).

In 1927 the great Chinese Christian preacher and writer, Watchman Nee, was struggling with issues of temptation and his sinful nature. One morning as he was sitting upstairs reading the book of Romans, he came to the words, "Knowing this, that our old man was crucified with Him" (6:6). For Nee, it was as if the words came to life on the page. He leapt from his chair, ran downstairs, and grabbed a kitchen worker by the hands. "Brother," he shouted. "Do you know that I have died?"

The worker stared in puzzlement. Nee explained, "Do you not know that Christ has died? Do you not know that I died with Him? Do you not know that my death is no less truly a fact than His?"

It was all Watchman Nee could do to keep himself from running through the streets of Shanghai, shouting about his death and new life. From that day on, his faith was confident and strong. His biographer wrote that it was impossible to say anything that might offend Nee. Why should he be offended? That Watchman Nee was long since dead![2]

Charles Spurgeon had his own way of explaining this amazing phenomenon of dying with Christ: "I suppose that, if you were to meet your old self, he would hardly know you, for you are so greatly altered. I daresay he would say to you, 'Come, old fellow, let us go to the theatre, or turn into this beer-shop, or let us go home, and find out some way of amusing ourselves.'

"You would reply, 'No, sir; I cut your acquaintance a long time ago, and I do not mean to have anything further to do with you, so you may go about your business as soon as you like. I am not what I was, for I have been crucified with Christ, and I am dead, and my life is hid with Christ in God.'"[3]

Those are great examples, but perhaps the best is a story having to do with the Reformation hero Martin Luther. One day Luther answered a knock at his door. "Does Dr. Martin Luther live here?" asked the visitor. "No," Luther answered, "he died. Christ lives here now."[4]

Ask the Lord to show you what this means! The old you is dead and in the grave; the new you is raised to walk in newness of life and to live victoriously for Christ. Our identity with His death cuts us off from our old life.

This is the basis now on which we can deal with Paul's three "withs."

Your Past Has Been Changed

Paul said, "If then you were raised with Christ .... You died" (Colossians 3:1, 3).

First, you have been raised up. In this sentence, the word "if" is better translated as "since." That's the way it's rendered in the New International Version: "Since, then, you have been raised with Christ."

This is a fact of history for every Christ-follower. Yes, we died in Christ, but we were also raised with Christ. Just as surely as Christ marched out of the tomb that first Easter Sunday, there was a day when David Jeremiah was spiritually resurrected through faith in Jesus Christ. At that moment, "old things have passed away; behold, all things have become new" (2 Corinthians 5:17).

Before that moment I was dead toward God; after that moment I was alive to Christ. The reign of sin over my life, which had existed until then, was broken. I was raised to newness of life.

One day the physical bodies of those who pass away in Christ will be resurrected, but the inner resurrection takes place at the moment of conversion. We begin to walk in newness of life.

Sharon Dutra's life was about as rough as it gets. She endured a miserable home life and was in and out of foster care. She was arrested again and again, addicted, married and divorced, living on the streets, looking for food in garbage cans. By age 29, she had been arrested thirteen times. In a crowded women's prison, she read the story of George H. Meyer, who had been the chauffeur and getaway driver for Al Capone. Meyer wrote of finding Christ, and his testimony penetrated her heart.

"Suddenly," she said, "I had remorse over my sin. I wept over what I had done to people and for my self-hatred. I asked God for forgiveness .... As I prayed, I felt God's grace wash over me. When I got up off the floor, I was a brand-new person."[5]

That was more than thirty years ago, and Sharon is still living in newness of life.

So are you, if you have been "raised with Christ."

Your Present Has Been Changed

Here's the second "with," and notice it is in the present tense: "Your life is hidden with Christ in God" (Colossians 3:3). The word "hidden" implies security. It's been awhile since I've sung this truth, but it was the focus of many of the hymns I've sung through the years. One of the greatest hymns says, "Rock of Ages, cleft for me, let me hide myself in Thee." Another hymn says, "Hidden in the hollow of His blessed hand, never foe can follow, never traitor stand."

All this points to our secure relationship. *The New Bible Commentary* says this implies our inner lives are hidden and secure, unable to be touched by anyone. We are protected. The world may rage against us, and our own circumstances may crumble, but our innermost spirits are safe and secure, hidden with Christ in God. In ways the world cannot see, we have inner spiritual resources to sustain us.

We are doubly secure. "With Christ in God" puts a double lock on the door of our security. This is a statement concerning our present situation with God.

"The language here is taken probably from treasure which is [hidden] or concealed in a place of security; and the idea is, that eternal life is an invaluable jewel ... which is laid up with Christ in heaven where God is. There it is safely deposited .... It is not left with us, or entrusted to our keeping—for then it might be lost .... Our eternal life, therefore, is as secure as it could possibly be made."[6]

An online handyman recently wrote an article about secret hiding places we've never thought about in our homes. Need to hide some money? Roll the bills up and stash them inside the spring bar that holds your toilet paper. Or the next time you empty a paint can, fill it up with valuables and put it back on the shelf with all the other cans. A soccer ball also makes a good hiding place. Let some of the air out, cut one of the seams with a utility knife, insert the items, and tuck the seam back into place.[7]

I don't know how well those ideas work. My problem would be forgetting the ingenious place where I decided to hide something. But I do know this. There is truly no safe hiding place in this world except in the security and safety of Jesus Christ. Jesus said, "And I give them eternal life, and they shall never perish; neither shall anyone snatch them out of My hand" (John 10:28).

Your Future Has Been Changed

Our Lord Jesus, then, has taken care of all that concerns our past—we were raised with Christ. He keeps us safe in the present—our lives are hidden with Christ. And the passage goes on to say He has plans for us in the future: "When Christ who is our life appears, then you also will appear with Him in glory" (Colossians 3:4).

Hollywood and Broadway constantly search for ways their characters can make dramatic entrances. Elected officials and their staff work hard to find ways to whip crowds into a frenzy as the politician comes onto the stage. The setting, music, leadup, dignitaries—everything is coordinated for maximum drama. Football teams work hard to maximize the emotion of running onto the field.

It's all dust and ashes compared to the moment of Christ's return.

We will see Him as few have imagined Him! So often people picture Jesus as a gentle Teacher and a tender Soul who died horribly but bravely. There's some truth to that, but it's far from the whole story. When He comes again we'll see Him in all His majesty, enveloped in clouds of glory, omnipotent in His power, and unyielding in His decrees. His face will shine as the sun, and "every knee should bow, of those in heaven, and of those on earth, and of those under the earth, and that every tongue should confess that Jesus Christ is Lord, to the glory of God the Father" (Philippians 2:10-11).

Mental images make a difference. Never forget! Jesus is risen, He sits at the right hand of the Father, and when we see Him, He will be revealed in all His magnificence. Even when the world seems to spin out of control, be calm; this is only how it seems. In reality, Almighty God is still on His throne, and, in the words of that old spiritual, "He's got the whole world in His hands."

Paul gives us this glorious message—it would be unbelievable if it weren't in Scripture—"When Christ who is our life appears, then you also will appear with Him in glory" (Colossians 3:4).

The apostle John said, "Beloved, now we are children of God; and it has not yet been revealed what we shall be, but we know that when He is revealed, we shall be like Him, for we shall see Him as He is" (1 John 3:2).

In the present we are hidden with Christ, but one day we will be revealed with Christ. Now that's something to set your mind on!

In Christ You Have a New Perspective

We could stop our study at this point and live with nothing but praise and thanksgiving. But there's more. Not only are you a new person in Christ. In Him you also have a new perspective. Look at these verses again: "If then you were raised with Christ, seek those things which are above, where Christ is, sitting at the right hand of God. Set your mind on things above, not on things on the earth" (Colossians 3:1-2).

Grammatically, these are imperatives or commands. They are not optional. The Lord longs for us—urges us, commands us—to do these things.

We Must Set Our Hearts on Things Above

Verse 1 tells us to "seek" those things that are above, and the New International Version rightly translates this, "Set your hearts on things above, where Christ is, seated at the right hand of God."

Have you ever set your heart on something? It means you are determined, you long for, yearn for, and hunger for something.

Dr. Anthony Viera of Duke University explained why he became a doctor. "As a boy growing up in a rural community," he said, "I set my heart on becoming a simple country doctor; that was the kind of doctor who I had seen in my community, who was really inspirational to me .... And complementing that was my fascination with TV's country doctors of the time— like Dr. Baker from 'Little House on the Prairie.'"

Although Dr. Viera now lives in a busy metropolitan area, he helps equip young physicians to practice in rural areas. He set his heart on a dream, and he pursued it with all his focus.[8]

Barbara Jo Rubin became the first female jockey to win a race at a U.S. thoroughbred track. She became enamored with horses and horse racing after watching the 1944 Elizabeth Taylor movie, *National Velvet*, about a girl who loves horses. "From that time on," said Rubin, "I set my heart on riding horses."[9]

When we set our heart on something, it motivates us, changes us, and energizes us. It makes our eyes shine, puts a spring in our step, and focuses our divided attention into a single, laser-intense direction.

In times such as these we have to look somewhere for answers. The psychologist tells us we should look within. The opportunist tells us we should look around. The optimist says we should look ahead, and the pessimist says we should look out. But God says we should look up—even when we feel down.[10]

In the midst of the chaos of our generation, we're to seek a perspective that can come only from God. Just as the compass points north, our entire perspective should be trained so it points toward the things of heaven.

Remember, we're citizens of that place toward which we are encouraged to set our hearts: "Our citizenship is in heaven, from which we also eagerly wait for the Savior, the Lord Jesus Christ" (Philippians 3:20).

Evangelist Vance Havner put it this way: "Christians are not citizens of earth trying to get to heaven, but citizens of heaven making their way through this world."[11]

We Must Set Our Minds on Things Above

The apostle Paul continued with a parallel thought in verse 2: "Set your minds on things above, not on earthly things" (NIV).

The phrase "set your minds" means "to focus one's thoughts on something." In other words, it's the mental discipline of directed thinking. We set our minds on taking a vacation. We set our minds on getting married. We can also set our minds on spiritual things. For whatever it's worth, that's one of the great takeaways of writing the Scripture in your own handwriting, as I like to do. It helps you to set your mind on heaven.

Is your mind occupied with spiritual truth, with the realities of things above?

When Paul wrote this statement, he used a verb tense that means "keep on doing this," as opposed to a one-time action. In other words, it's not, "think about heaven at this moment." It's "keep on keeping your mind immersed in God and His Word, all the time." This is a discipline too few of us have mastered: the art of heaven-based thinking. Some call it practicing the presence of God.

That's the positive command, but it is accompanied by a warning against the negative: "Set your mind on things above, not on things on the earth" (Colossians 3:2).

Paul isn't telling us to forego the physical challenges and chores of everyday life while we sit and ruminate on heaven and angels. God wants you to take care of earthly business. We live in this physical world, and we should do everything, including everyday responsibilities, as unto the Lord.

That's why it's okay to buy a car, to invest in a home, and to enjoy your hobbies. But we don't set our hearts and minds on perishable things because they will pass away. The eternal things have our allegiance.

Learn to say with the psalmist: "Whom have I in heaven but You? And there is none upon earth that I desire besides You" (Psalm 73:25).

This focus is not so much on heaven as a place, though that is a wonderful thing to think about, but on heaven as a spiritual reality which controls our total motivation. By deliberately and daily committing ourselves to the values of the heavenly kingdom, believers seek that which is above. This is to be our lifestyle and thought pattern as followers of Christ.

We're called to be like a man who had to travel from his home in New York to London. He didn't like to travel. He wasn't eager to be away from his family or his company or his church. He reluctantly went to London, but he made sure his watch stayed on New York time. Whenever he looked at his watch, he knew what was going on back home—when the kids were going to school, when his wife was picking them up, when they were going to church, when they went to bed. Though doing business in London, he kept his mind on the things going on at home.

I can tell that story with authenticity because I never change the time on my watch. I make mental calculations, but I want to keep my mind on things at home. In the same way, we must keep our ticking hearts set to God's clocks, and we must set our minds on things above.

Train yourself to think biblically, to think in heavenly terms, and to practice the presence of God.

In Christ You Have New Priorities

Let's review. In Christ you're a new person, and in Christ you have a new perspective. As we continue more deeply into the verses that follow, we find that in Christ we also have—or should have—new priorities. As we focus our minds on things above, our values will change. Paul becomes very practical as he shows us how these heavenly habits have earthly implications. And he starts with the troublesome subject of sexual impurity.

Sexual Discipline

Colossians 3:5-7 says, "Therefore put to death your members which are on the earth: fornication, uncleanness, passion, evil desire, and covetousness, which is idolatry. Because of these things the wrath of God is coming upon the sons of disobedience, in which you yourselves once walked when you lived in them."

In the Greek language, the phrase "put to death" is very strong. In fact, in some translations this phrase is rendered "mortify"—the word from which we get *mortician*. When it comes to the sins of the flesh, we need to be spiritual morticians and bury them in the ground.

In verses 5 through 7, Paul gave the Colossians a list of five things they were to ruthlessly eliminate from their lives followed by one reason they were to put those things to death.

"*Fornication* refers to sexual immorality in general. *Uncleanness* means 'lustful impurity that is connected with luxury and loose living.' [*Passion*] describes a state of mind that excites sexual impurity. The person who cultivates this kind of appetite can always find opportunity to satisfy it. [*Evil desires*] means 'base, evil desires.'"[12]

Attached to this list of sins is a warning: "Because of these things the wrath of God is coming upon the sons of disobedience, in which you yourselves once walked when you lived in them" (Colossians 3:6-7).

Why are these behaviors and desires to be put to death? Because they are the things God hates; they are the things that make Him angry.

Finally, Paul reminds the Colossians of their past. They were once filled and dominated by evil desires. They once walked in all kinds of sensual sins. But no longer. God had changed them, and now God would use their own effort to continually change them.

My dear friend, be careful about those vulnerable moments. Beware those moments of fatigue and insecurity when the devil will speak to your weakness. Set your mind on things above and remember what Paul said: "But among you there must not be even a hint of sexual immorality" (Ephesians 5:3, NIV).

Mental Discipline

That requires mental discipline, which brings us to the next phrase in verse 5: "Therefore put to death ... covetousness, which is idolatry" (Colossians 3:5).

Covetousness is subtle because it's violated totally in the mind. It's the invisible violation no one else sees. You and I can have our act completely together on the outside, but inside we can be agonizing over, lusting after, and being consumed by the desire to have what someone else has.

Warren Wiersbe wrote, "Covetousness is the sin of always wanting more, whether it be more things or more pleasures. The covetous person is never satisfied with what he has, and he is usually envious of what other people have."[13]

Covetousness is an attitude, and it's an enemy to the sufficiency of Christ. It's idolatry because it raises a rival object of worship. The writer of Hebrews says we're to replace coveting with contentment: "Let your conduct be without covetousness; be content with such things as you have" (Hebrews 13:5).

Coveting is idolatry, the worship of a false god. Contentment is praise, the worship of the true God.

Social Discipline

Let's keep pressing on into this passage. Colossians 3:8 says: "But now you yourselves are to put off all these: anger, wrath, malice."

Expositor John Phillips points out that the phrase "put off" implies taking off garments. The idea is stripping away, removing, shedding. He used this graphic illustration:

> In 1665, the Great Plague raged throughout the city of London. Those who could afford to fled the city. Those who remained lived in terror. Because the people who remained in London did not know what caused the plague, the most elementary hygienic precautions were ignored. People in the city continued to send parcels of used clothing, often the property of the dead, to poorer relatives and relief agencies. Even clothes stripped off of the bodies of the plague victims were dispatched.
>
> Imagine a family's receiving such a parcel and proudly and gratefully putting on clothes much better in quality and style to their usual everyday wear. Then they discovered these attractive new garments had come from the plague houses. With what horror would they strip them off and consign them to the fire! It is with such horror we should strip off the old man and his deeds; he has the plague![14]

We're to work hard to peel off the attitudes of anger, wrath, and malice that our personalities sometimes wear around like costumes.

Anger is the emotion that we try to keep below the surface, wrath is when it suddenly bursts out, and malice refers to the ongoing resentment that often seeks to harm others in some way.

Many people who have a beautiful smile and a successful life have been enslaved by an angry attitude. Many media reports say this is true of actor Tom Cruise. His former manager, Eileen Berlin, said, "Tommy had a terrible temper. He harbored a lot of anger at his natural father. He was moody and would get angry in a snap of your fingers .... It was like something was smoldering, and it would boil up and explode. I put it down to his insecurity. I presented him with ... all his publicity articles from teen magazines for his 19th birthday. He screamed, 'I don't want to be in the teen mags.' He had told me he considered himself an adult, not a teen idol. He threw the album hard at me, and it hit me on the cheek."[15]

I'm not singling out one actor. What Eileen Berlin said about Cruise could be said about lots of famous, infamous, and ordinary people. In fact, without the work of God's Holy Spirit in our lives helping us, the clothing of anger, wrath, and malice are exceedingly hard to remove. It's like they're attached to us with a Velcro stronger than we are.

But when Christ is in us and with us, we have His help in working on these attitudes and bringing discipline into our lives.

Vocal Discipline

You can see the progress of Paul's thoughts in verses 5 through 9. The next personal issue he tackles is the way we talk—our tongues, our speech. He said, "But now you yourselves are to put off all these ... blasphemy, filthy language out of your mouth. Do not lie to one another, since you have put off the old man with his deeds" (Colossians 3:8-9).

Blasphemy can be directed at God or at someone else. It means demeaning or being irreverent or reviling toward someone or their reputation.

Filthy language is obscenity (taking body parts or physical processes and turning them into objectionable speech) or profanity (taking scriptural names and words and using them as swear words).

I recall when you never heard obscenity or profanity on television, and now even children's programming suddenly has bad language at times. A friend of mine said his three-year-old great-grandson opened the door the other day and said, "It's [blanking] cold out there!"

"Where did you hear that word?" said his shocked mother.

You can believe they tracked down the source and dealt with the matter, while also giving the three-year-old a helpful little talk about words that shouldn't be spoken.

It's not simply a matter of keeping our lips free from curses. It's a matter of using our tongues to build up others and to proclaim the glory of God with our words.

Dr. Criswell graphically described the potential for evil that resides in the tongue when he wrote:

There are many people who have never set fire to
a man burned at the stake; they have never clapped
their hands at the shrieks of those who in agony
were being torn apart by a ferocious lion in some
colosseum. There are people who have never beat the
drums to drown out the agonizing cry of those who
were offered to the fiery god of Moloch; but there
are people without number who assassinate friends,
neighbors, and acquaintances by untrue tale-bearing,
vicious and evil words ... I do not think there is
anyone of us but has felt the sting of unkind words.[16]

Curtis Vaughan adds these insightful thoughts about the
tongue: "It can sway men to violence, or it can move them to
the noblest actions. It can instruct the ignorant, encourage
the dejected, comfort the sorrowing, and soothe the dying.
Or it can crush the human spirit, destroy reputations, spread
distrust and hate, and bring nations to the brink of war."[17]

We can use our words to bring life or bring death. We make
the choice.

In Christ You Have a New Purpose

As wonderful as Colossians 3 is, we haven't mined all its
depths. In Christ we are a new person—past, present, and
future. In Him we have a new perspective, setting both our
hearts and our minds on things above. In Him we have new
priorities including sexual, mental, social, and vocal discipline.

But there's more. In Christ we have a new purpose.

Look at Colossians 3:10-11: "And have put on the new man who is renewed in knowledge according to the image of Him who created him, where there is neither Greek nor Jew, circumcised nor uncircumcised, barbarian, Scythian, slave nor free, but Christ is all and in all."

The phrase "put on" is the opposite of "put off." We take off the soiled garments of sinfulness, and we put on the splendid coat of a new person who is beginning to wear the very personality of Jesus Christ—the image of Him who created us and made us now, the image of the One who is all and in all.

One commentary said, "Believers are to discard their old, repulsive habits like a set of worn-out clothes. They are then to adorn themselves with the kind of behaviors that will make them well dressed and appropriately fashionable for the new way of life God has given them."[18]

The New Man is Jesus Christ, whose identity every believer takes as their own, and in whom there can be no division—because He is all in all.

Randy Alcorn wrote one of the best explanations for Christlikeness I've ever heard: "People had only to look at Jesus to see what God is like. People today should only have to look at us to see what Jesus is like."[19]

Paul tells us in Colossians 3:11 that if we, as Christians, develop the disciplines he has listed for us, the renewal of our lives will be so radical we'll remove relationship barriers. Racial barriers will be gone (Greek or Jew); religious barriers will be gone (circumcised or uncircumcised); cultural barriers will be gone (barbarian or Scythian); social barriers will be gone (slave or free).

Maybe your life used to be marked by fornication, evil desires, impurity, and uncleanness. Maybe you were greedy and angry. Maybe your anger and malice controlled you. Perhaps you lied about others.

Here's the point: Christ doesn't do those things! And since you are in Christ, you don't have to do those things anymore. You can take off all of those habits and desires. And instead, each day, you can dress yourself with "the new man." You can focus all of your effort and attention on who you really are: a pure, clean, generous, patient, honest believer in Christ!

The football world lost a hero last year when Richard Price passed away at age 81. He was born in Vicksburg, Mississippi, in 1939 and was a high school football standout. At Ole Miss, he helped lead his team to three straight bowl game wins and two national championships. Later he was drafted by the Oakland Raiders and was inducted into the Mississippi Sports Hall of Fame.

In an interview with the *Vicksburg Press* not long before his death, Price said, "In the environment I grew up in, I knew I had to get out of Vicksburg. There was only one way to get out for me and that was to get a scholarship. I trained hard, and I worked hard and then I married the most wonderful girl in the world. I changed as a husband, but I hadn't changed inside as a person."

Then came the greatest crisis of his life. His seven-year-old daughter suffered a serious head injury in a horse riding accident. "For the first time in my life I was totally helpless," Price recalled. "For three days, she wasn't supposed to make it through the night."

That's when the Great Physician stepped into the picture.

"God worked on me that night," said Price. "I gave my life to Jesus Christ. My life is to serve him."

Price's little daughter was in a coma for six weeks, but she eventually made a complete recovery. "I live every day to be a good husband, to be a good father, to be a servant of Jesus Christ. That's what I want to do, until the day I die. Jesus Christ changed me."[20]

Jesus Christ changed me!

What a testimony in four words! And in a sense, those four words sum up the message of Colossians 3:1-11. The opening verses tell us we are in Christ and "with Christ," and Christ is in us. At the end of this passage, we're reminded that "Christ is all and in all."

That means He is sufficient. He is enough! There is no need to look elsewhere. He is what the world needs more than ever before! He can save us from our sins and He can save us from ourselves. Receive Him! Love Him! Follow Him! Worship Him! Fellowship with Him! And share Him with others!

CHAPTER 7

The Christian's Dress Code

COLOSSIANS 3:12-17

IN THE 1961 FILM, *BREAKFAST AT TIFFANY'S*, AUDREY Hepburn played a young lady who fell in love with a struggling writer, and the plot unfolded in a way that gained the movie five Academy Award nominations and six Grammy nominations. Decades passed and not long ago, the black Givenchy dress Hepburn wore in the film was auctioned off for over $800,000, making it one of the most expensive dresses of all time.[1]

Few of us have a budget like that. Yet even when we shop in the bargain basement, clothes are becoming more expensive. We spend hundreds of hours and thousands of dollars each year on clothing. But have you ever stopped to ask what the Bible says about the topic?

It's a fascinating study.

At the beginning of Genesis, Adam and Eve didn't need to spend much on their wardrobe. But after they sinned, what did they do? They sewed fig leaves together to cover their nakedness and shame. God could have struck them dead or shamed them for their sin. Instead, He covered them in grace and gave them animal skins for garments (Genesis 3:21).

Later in the book of Genesis, Jacob presented his beloved son Joseph with a robe of many colors (Genesis 37:3). The clothes were later stained with blood as Joseph was swept off to Egypt. But later we see him in garments of fine linen when he was released from prison to become a leader in Egypt (Genesis 41:42).

Clothes played important roles in the story of Saul and David, the life of the high priest, and the ministries of Elijah and Elisha.

In Psalms, David sang about how God removes our tattered sackcloth and clothes us with gladness (Psalm 30:11). Isaiah rejoiced because God had clothed him with the garments of salvation (Isaiah 61:10).

When John the Baptist came, he was distinctly dressed in camel's hair, with a leather belt around his waist.

Then history's greatest miracle happened. Jesus—the One who clothes Himself in glory—took on flesh and was wrapped in swaddling clothes.

From the time of His birth until His death and resurrection, the subject of clothing often appeared in Jesus's ministry. For example, on one occasion He told a story about a prodigal son who was covered in pigsty manure. When the boy returned home, his father embraced his son and covered him with his best robe (Luke 15:21-23).

On another occasion, Jesus confronted a demon-possessed man known for his uncontrollable madness, his graveyard home, and his constant nakedness. Then the demoniac met Jesus. The demon was cast out, and we're told that the townspeople were amazed to see the man "clothed and in his right mind" (Luke 8:35).

As Jesus went to the cross, He was mocked, wrapped in a purple robe, and crowned with a thorny diadem (Mark 15:17). And then He was taken to Golgotha, where He was stripped, suspended between heaven and earth, and nailed to a tree to die.

The Bible says, "And they divided His garments and cast lots" (Luke 23:34).

At that moment Christ, by wearing our shame and nakedness, secured eternal life for His people, who would be clothed in Him forever. Because of Christ's work on the cross, believers are now clothed with His righteousness (Isaiah 61:10).

Now, we are instructed to wear the armor of God (Ephesians 6:10-20; 1 Thessalonians 5:8) and clothe ourselves with Christ as we look forward to the resurrection of our bodies—the day when we will be clothed with immortality (1 Corinthians 15:53).

As Cade Campbell says so well:

The storyline of the Bible begins with the tattered attempt to sew a wardrobe out of our own efforts, to piece together fig leaves to undo the damage that we'd done. But the story of the Bible ends ... with sons and daughters of Adam and Eve living in paradise again, fully in the presence of God, and reigning forever in the wardrobe of redemption .... [There] the redeemed who live into eternity as those who are "clothed in white garments" whose names will never be blotted out from the Book of Life (Revelation 3:5), because they have "washed their robes and made them white in the blood of the Lamb" (Revelation 7:14).[2]

Against this broad background, I'd like to take you to Colossians 3:12-17, where the apostle Paul tells us what it means to clothe ourselves with Christ. Take a moment to read these verses:

Therefore, as the elect of God, holy and beloved, put on tender mercies, kindness, humility, meekness, longsuffering; bearing with one another, and forgiving one another, if anyone has a complaint against another; even as Christ forgave you, so you also must do. But above all these things put on love, which is the bond of perfection. And let the peace of God rule in your hearts, to which also you were called in one body; and be thankful. Let the word of Christ dwell in you richly in all wisdom, teaching and admonishing one another in psalms and hymns and spiritual songs, singing with grace in your hearts to the Lord. And whatever you do in word or deed, do all in the name of the Lord Jesus, giving thanks to God the Father through Him.

Receive the Grace of Christ

Verse 12 begins with a sort of preamble to this section: "Therefore, as the elect of God, holy and beloved." In other words, we're to remember we are elect, holy, and loved by God. The focus in verse 12 is not on what we can do for God, but what He has done for us.

God doesn't love His people because of what we have accomplished or how we compare to others. He loves us just because He does! Paul wrote: "He chose us in Him before the foundation of the world, that we should be holy and without blame before Him in love" (Ephesians 1:4).

Paul wanted the Colossians to know that God had chosen them, but he also wanted them to dwell on the fact that they were set apart by God. That is the meaning of the word "holy."

"Beloved" could be translated as "dearly loved." It's a powerful word that occurs more than one hundred times in the Bible. This is the word God the Father used to express His love for God the Son at His baptism: "This is My beloved Son, in whom I am well pleased" (Matthew 3:17).

So our first obligation is to receive the grace of God and relish it. Appreciate it. View all of life through its lens.

The website for the magazine *Gentleman's Quarterly* recently ran an article on the popularity of colored sunglasses. It's not just brown or blue or gray lenses anymore. You can choose colors to play off the rest of your outfit or to express a mood or the style you're feeling. While they don't block out as much of the sun's rays, most colored lenses provide some UV protection, and there are other benefits. Yellow lenses can reduce eyestrain. Red lenses are said to have a calming effect, the article said.

According to the magazine, the important thing is this: "What color do you want to see the world in?"[3]

I want to see myself and my world in tones of grace and through the lens of the mercy and salvation of Christ.

To begin our wardrobe, let's put on the glasses of grace!

Put on the Character of Christ

Now for the rest of our ensemble. Colossians 3:12-14 says: "Put on tender mercies, kindness, humility, meekness, longsuffering; bearing with one another, and forgiving one another, if anyone has a complaint against another; even as Christ forgave you, so you also must do. But above all these things put on love, which is the bond of perfection."

In the last chapter, I told you about the things we were to strip away from our lives—to put off. Now, the Lord takes us into the divine wardrobe and gives us a list of virtues to put on, as if we were putting on clothing.

Each of these virtues involves personal relationships. They are qualities of character necessary for connection and unity within the Church. They show us how it's possible to get along with one another, and they represent, in essence, the character of Christ.

Each of these traits adorned the life of our Lord. So when Paul told the Colossians to "put on" these virtues, he was telling them to put on the character of Christ. In other words, he is opening to us the wardrobe of Jesus. He is asking us to answer the question: What would Jesus wear?

Put on His Tender Mercies

The first item we come to are "tender mercies." That's the feeling within our innermost selves that moves us to compassion. Colossians 3:12 says, "Put on tender mercies." J. B. Phillips translated this, "be merciful in action." The New International Version simply says, "clothe yourselves with compassion."

This phrase appears only twelve times in the New King James Version, usually in the Old Testament describing God's attitude of tender mercy toward us. Here in Colossians 3:12 we have the only time this word is used in the New Testament. It's as if Paul is saying, "We all want God to treat us with tender mercy, why not treat others the same way?"

William Barclay wrote about the need for mercy in the ancient world, but he could have just as easily written the same words about us today: "If there was one thing the ancient world needed, it was mercy. The sufferings of animals meant nothing. The physically handicapped and the weak did not survive. There was no provision for the elderly. The treatment of anyone suffering from mental illness was unfeeling. Christianity brought mercy into this world. It is not too much to say that everything that has been done for the elderly, the sick, the weak in body and in mind, animals, children and women has been done through the inspiration of Christianity."[4]

Compassion is the most powerful tool in the world for melting hatred. It's like a blowtorch that melts icy attitudes. The Christian quality of compassion has changed the world again and again. For instance, while Jesus was preaching in Jerusalem, the citizens of Rome were piling up unwanted babies and abandoning them at the base of the Columna Lactaria. If a child was sickly or unwanted, the baby was simply left to die at the base of this column. Dr. Alvin Schmidt wrote, "In neither Greek nor Roman literature can one find any feelings of guilt related to abandoning children."

That all changed as the Gospel spread. Clement of Alexandria, a church father in Egypt, condemned the Romans for abandoning children, as did the church father, Tertullian. But the Christians did more than preach against this evil. They began taking in abandoned children, showing them kindness, and saving their lives.

Dr. Schmidt wrote, "In spite of the many severe persecutions that Christians endured for three centuries, they did not relent in promoting the sanctity of human life. They saw child abandonment as a form of murder, and their tenacious efforts eventually produced results."[5]

Both as a movement and among all of us as individual followers, the work of Jesus Christ is the extension of the compassion of the Savior Himself.

Put on His Kindness

Next, Paul tells us to put on the parallel attitude of kindness (Colossians 3:12). In the closely-related letter to the Ephesians, Paul instructed us to "be kind one to another" (Ephesians 4:32).

You probably know that every December *TIME* magazine announces its Person of the Year, with the person's picture on the cover along with an extended article about how that person's life impacted the world for good, or sometimes for bad. The editors try to determine who has made a difference in history.

Did you know the magazine also has a Kid of the Year? Last year, it was Orion Jean, an eleven-year-old Texas boy. His life mission is to make the world a kinder place. He said, "For me, it can take on so many different forms from just smiling at somebody or holding the door, or even donating food to the local food bank or giving away old toys that you don't need."

Jean has also won the National Kindness Speech Contest, and he used the five hundred dollar prize to create an organization in his town devoted to kindness. He and his organization have sponsored a toy drive, a book drive, and a food drive for the hungry. Jean gets his inspiration watching the local news, where he spots needs. Then he tries to figure out how they can be met.[6]

"In a time when it seems nothing is in order, one thing will always stay the same and that is kindness," said Orion.[7]

Paul encouraged us to think of kindness as a lifestyle, like a piece of clothing we wear all the time. It's the attitude of wanting to bless others, to lift their spirits, to meet their needs—and to do so in Jesus' Name.

Put on His Humility

If we don't look carefully, we may overlook another garment in the wardrobe of Christ because it calls no attention to itself. It's the apron of humility. Humility is sometimes called the quiet virtue.

Some in the Colossian church had a counterfeit humility. Paul described the false teachers who had invaded the area as people who delighted in "false humility" (Colossians 2:18, 2:23). It does no good to pretend to be humble. Genuine humility can't be manufactured by our personalities; it must be imported into us by the Man of Galilee.

On nine separate occasions, the Bible warns us against being wise in our own eyes (Proverbs 3:7; 12:15; 26:5, 12, 16; 28:11; Isaiah 5:21; Romans 11:25; 12:16). When we're wise in our own eyes, we stop listening; we stop asking questions; we stop trying to learn. We think we "know it all," and arrogance and pride take over in our lives.

One day some years ago, former football coach Tony Dungy picked up the phone and listened as a friend anguished over his troubled son. "My son is depressed and he talks about ending his own life. Could you call him and find a way to help him?"

Dungy, who had faced such a tragedy with his own son, agreed. Calling the young man, Dungy said, "My name is Tony. Your dad asked me to talk to you." He went on to tell the young man how much he had suffered when his own son, James, had taken his life. "You know, son," said Tony, "I don't know why God allowed my son to die. But maybe it was so that I could talk to you and tell you, 'Don't do that to your daddy.'"

Coach Dungy spoke to the young man every day for a week, and the long conversations helped the troubled youth. Finally the young man said he was doing better, and he agreed to get the help he needed. The two stayed in touch, and one day the young man asked, "Tony, what do you do for a living?"

"I'm a football coach," Dungy replied.

"College or high school football?"

Dungy said, "I coach the Indianapolis Colts."

Only then did the young man know he had been talking to one of the best-known and most-respected leaders in the world of sports. Tony's entire focus had been helping the young man, and he would have done the same had he been an obscure and unknown man. His humility wasn't on show. It was just there.[8]

Put on His Meekness

The next garment Paul suggests is meekness, as he continues in Colossians 3:12: "Therefore, as the elect of God, holy and beloved, put on tender mercies, kindness, humility, meekness."

We don't use the word "meekness" a lot today, but it is a wonderful word. It is not a synonym for weakness. The only thing the two words have in common is that they rhyme. Most newer translations render this word "gentleness."

Outside of three major American cities is an organization called The Gentle Barn. It not only rescues animals, but it also takes the gentlest of those animals and makes them available for cuddling, holding, and enjoying. The animals minister in remarkable ways to troubled children and adults. At-risk youngsters, people recovering from addictions, war veterans, and others can go there to spend time hugging a cow, petting a goat, snuggling against a sheep, brushing a horse, or holding a turkey. Something about the gentleness of these rescued animals helps heal anxiety and promote well-being.[9]

I grew up in farming territory, and I know something about the strength of a horse or a cow. Some horses bite, and a cow's tail can sting like a whip. A gentle animal is no less strong, but its strength is clothed in geniality.

This is actually a biblical connection. The Greek word translated "meekness" in Colossians 3:12 was the same word used in antiquity to tame a horse to a bit and bridle.[10] We're living in a world of snarling, irritable, snapping people. The follower of Christ must be under the Master's control—strong, yet gentle. John Wooden said, "It takes strength inside to be gentle on the outside."[11]

The two greatest examples of meekness in the Bible are Jesus and Moses. "Christ came not as a domineering and abusive King but as a good and gentle Lord. He descended gently into our world in Bethlehem, grew in wisdom and stature in Nazareth, taught with toughness and tenderness in Galilee, and rode into Jerusalem 'humble, and mounted on a donkey' (Matt. 21:5) to lay down his life."[12]

Second only to Jesus, the Bible says the next meekest man was Moses (Numbers 12:3). "He was a commander-in-chief, a general who led the children of Israel out of the land of bondage to their Promised Land. He stood down Pharaoh face to face in his own palace, when Pharaoh was the most powerful ruler on earth in his day. Moses was a mighty man of valor. Meekness is not being timid, soft-spoken, insecure, or shy ....

"Meekness is incredible strength under control ....

"The best example of strength under control is what happens when a trainer takes a wild horse and 'breaks' that stallion so he can be ridden and be useful. His strength isn't altered or taken away—it's domesticated and channeled for good."[13]

So meekness is using our God-given abilities in a way that doesn't overwhelm or overpower others. Meekness doesn't run people over. It's strength under control for the benefit of others.

Put on His Patience

There's another layer of clothing we need to wear. The list in Colossians 3:12-13 says, "Tender mercies, kindness, humility, meekness, longsuffering; bearing with one another."

"Longsuffering" is the opposite of revenge. Literally, the word means "long-temper."

Warren Wiersbe explained, "The short-tempered person speaks and acts impulsively and lacks self-control. When a person is longsuffering, he can put up with provoking people or circumstances without retaliating. It is good to be able to get angry, for this is a sign of holy character. But it is wrong to get angry quickly at the wrong things and for the wrong reasons."[14]

Notice the follow-up phrase "bearing with." Here Paul was admitting it can be hard to get along with certain people in the church. Sometimes we have to put up with difficult people in the church or elsewhere, people we would not normally choose to associate with.

Kent Hughes told a story about this that made me laugh. He wrote, "In the days before smoking was banned from airplanes and there were smoking and non-smoking sections on the plane, a man started to light a cigar. The flight attendant told him that he was not allowed to smoke a cigar unless it was alright with the other person in the immediate area. So she asked the lady sitting next to him, 'Do you object to his smoking?' 'I absolutely detest cigars,' was the reply. The flight attendant then spoke to a young man who was seated near the front of the cabin and came back to report that he would not mind sitting next to a cigar-smoker. As the cigar-smoking man walked forward to his new seat, his former seatmate, the boisterous woman, turned to the flight attendant and said, 'I've been married to that man for thirty years and I still can't stand his awful cigars.'"[15]

Everyone in the world has some habit or trait that rubs us the wrong way. When we become tired and irritable, we're prone to react in ways that damage our relationships. Most of us aren't naturally patient. Show me a toddler who is patient! In fact, I believe we're born with a mood of impatience. But we're born again to become patient people who bear with one another without becoming rude and surly.

The preacher, A. B. Simpson, said, "Beloved, have you ever thought that someday you will not have anything to try you, or anyone to vex you again? There will be no opportunity in heaven to learn or to show the spirit of patience, forbearance, and longsuffering. If you are to practice these things, it must be now."

Put on His Forgiveness

We're not surprised to find the next item on Paul's list. He goes on to say, "Forgiving one another, if anyone has a complaint against another; even as Christ forgave you, so you also must do" (Colossians 3:13-14).

Paul moved beyond simply enduring or putting up with other believers. In these verses, he reminded the Colossians they should also forgive one another. Instead of complaining against someone, Paul said to forgive them.

In the New Testament, Christ provides both the possibility and pattern of forgiveness for believers: "And be kind to one another, tenderhearted, forgiving one another, even as God in Christ forgave you" (Ephesians 4:32).

How did God forgive us? For Christ's sake, He forgave us unconditionally. He forgave us freely. He didn't say, "I'll forgive, but I won't forget!" The Bible says when He forgave, He threw our sins into the deepest part of the sea (Micah 7:19). As Corrie ten Boom said, He put up a sign saying, "No fishing!" He put our sin behind His back, as far as the east is from the west (Psalm 103:12). That is how we are to forgive—just as we are forgiven.

John Phillips wrote, "In one of his sermons, D.L. Moody used to picture the Lord saying to Peter, 'Go hunt up the man who put the crown of thorns on my head and tell him that I love him. Tell him he can have a crown in my kingdom, one without a thorn. Find the man who spat in my face and preach the gospel to him. Tell him that I forgive him and that I died to save him. Find the man who thrust the spear into my side and tell him that there is a quicker way into my heart.' That is how the Lord Jesus has forgiven us. Now it is our turn."[16]

Let me ask you something. Have you been forgiven by God through Jesus Christ? Are your sins nailed to His cross? All your sins of omission, commission, and disposition erased by the acid power of His blood?

Yes? Then why should we harbor resentful attitudes toward others? Toward someone in our home? Why do we carry around grudges? We are to forgive *because* God has forgiven us, and we're to forgive *as* He has forgiven us. When we do so, renewed blessings come into our lives.

Put on His Love

And now we come to the zenith of Paul's instruction in this passage: "But above all these things put on love, which is the bond of perfection" (Colossians 3:14).

Jesus taught, "The first of all the commandments is: 'Hear, O Israel, the Lord our God, the Lord is one. And you shall love the Lord your God with all your heart, with all your soul, with all your mind, and with all your strength.' This is the first commandment. And the second, like it, is this: 'You shall love your neighbor as yourself.' There is no other commandment greater than these" (Mark 12:29-31).

Paul wrote, "And now abide faith, hope, love, these three; but the greatest of these is love" (1 Corinthians 13:13).

One Bible teacher said, "Love is not so much a garment to be put on over the other garments, but rather the golden thread running through the entire wardrobe. What is your theme in dress? Throughout the entire wardrobe of a holy life the consistent theme is love."[17]

Biblical love isn't simply a feeling. It is something we do. C. S. Lewis said, "Do not waste time bothering whether you 'love' your neighbor; act as if you did." In other words, no matter our feelings at the moment, we must love our neighbors with the love of Christ, and let our feelings catch up to our obedience.

Tender mercies, kindness, humility, meekness, and longsuffering only attain their power when they are empowered and motivated by love.

Submit to the Peace of Christ

Let's sum up what we've learned so far in Colossians 3. When we receive the grace of God, we're able to put on the character of Christ. Like layering clothing on a chilly day, we're called to go into the cold world around us dressed in tender mercies, kindness, humility, meekness, patience, forgiveness, and love.

What's next?

Colossians 3:15 is a wonderful verse. It's a command, but there's a promise tucked into the command: "And let the peace of God rule in your hearts, to which also you were called in one body; and be thankful."

While many translations render this phrase "the peace of God," the more literal translation is "the peace of Christ." This is the peace that comes from Christ, the One who said, "Peace I leave with you, My peace I give to you; not as the world gives do I give to you. Let not your heart be troubled, neither let it be afraid" (John 14:27).

This peace is to rule in our hearts. The word "rule" is the translation of a Greek term found only here in the New Testament. It means literally "to sit as umpire." We all know the decision of the umpire is final.

William Barclay explained: "If the peace of Jesus Christ is the umpire in anyone's heart, then, when feelings clash and we are pulled in two directions at the same time, the decision of

Christ will keep us in the way of love, and the Church will remain the one body it is meant to be. The way to right action is to appoint Jesus Christ as the one who decides between the conflicting emotions in our hearts; and, if we accept his decisions, we cannot go wrong."[18]

There have been many times in my life when I was trying to decide what to do between two things that seemed equal. The thing that helped me make the right decision was when I found I could say: "I don't have peace in my heart about that," or "God has really given me a sense of peace about that."

June DePriest has taught the Bible for many years in Jackson, Mississippi. In her book, *A Resting Place*, she wrote about the time when, as a young wife and mother, she learned her husband, Joe, had serious heart disease. He wasn't likely to live. For days afterward, June had her daily quiet time of Bible study and prayer in her blue rocking chair. Some mornings all she did was cry. Other days she would memorize needed verses and passages. But her fears were always near the surface. Then one morning, she stood up and made a personal decision: "Lord, whether Joe lives or whether Joe dies, I will love You and serve You." For her, it was an altar experience.

"After my altar experience, did I stay at perfect peace? I didn't, but I had a better understanding of how to live at peace," June wrote. "It's a choice that must be made countless times a day. A troubled spirit is a good indication that we are not trusting God; we are mulling things over and over."

She continued, "A picture can't be painted of God's peace. Money can't buy it , nor can it be found if we search the world for it. But it's God's promise and His gift for us."[19]

Make it a priority to let the peace of Christ rule in your heart.

Dwell on the Word of Christ

Paul's words continue to cascade through Colossians 3 like a series of waterfalls. He next wrote, "Let the word of Christ dwell in you richly in all wisdom, teaching and admonishing one another in psalms and hymns and spiritual songs, singing with grace in your hearts to the Lord" (Colossians 3:16).

Remember, Paul was not writing to a single individual here, but to a congregation. The New Living Translation helps us see this more clearly: "Let the message about Christ, in all its richness, fill your lives. Teach and counsel each other with all the wisdom he gives. Sing psalms and hymns and spiritual songs to God with thankful hearts."

Verse 16 is one of the few New Testament verses that explicitly describe what a Christian worship service should look like. Paul's point is simple: The message about Christ should be at the center of their worship services. It should dwell there. It should take up permanent residence there. It is one thing for you to be in the Word; it is quite another thing for the Word to be in you!

Not only that, but we should be using the Scripture to teach and counsel each other, and there should also be lots of singing "with grace in your hearts to the Lord."

One pastor calls church singing "'take-home theology,' because the best songs we sing together give us an easily memorisable, deeply biblical summary of important biblical truths. When we sing, we're digging deep roots in the word."[20]

In other words, I'm not the only one preaching and teaching the Word of God on Saturday night and Sunday morning in my church. All the worshipers are as they sing. We're singing not just to the Lord but for the Lord. We're teaching and admonishing those around us.

Last year, Sheriff Jody Greene faced a dilemma. A Bible verse was posted on the wall of his office—Philippians 4:13: "I can do all things through Christ which strengtheneth me" (KJV). An atheistic group asked him to remove the verse, claiming it alienated citizens who were not religious. Greene refused. He said in a social media post: "The verse is one of my favorite Bible verses, and it seemed fitting for all the adversity I have had to endure. It is very motivational to me and my staff. Here at the Sheriff's Office, we work hard in everything that we do. Before we execute a search warrant, or any service that puts our people in immediate harm's way, we ALWAYS go to the Lord with a group prayer. ALWAYS."

"We need more Jesus and less politics," he said.[21]

I hope Sheriff Greene is able to keep that verse on his wall. At the same time, I'm appalled at how many churches are minimizing the Word of God in their services. I'm alarmed at how many Christians go for days without opening their Bibles. Let's write the Word of God on the walls of our hearts and let it dwell in us richly. Let's let it echo within the walls of our churches and fill our congregations. And let's shout it from the mountaintop because the Bible is our best weapon in fighting all the adversity we have to endure in this world.

Live for the Name of Christ

Let's press on to one final verse in this passage: "And whatever you do in word or deed, do all in the name of the Lord Jesus, giving thanks to God the Father through Him" (Colossians 3:17). This is one of a handful of "whatever you do" verses in the Bible. Have you ever noticed how Scripture embraces this phrase?

- "Commit to the Lord whatever you do, and he will establish your plans" (Proverbs 16:3, NIV).

- "Plan carefully what you do, and whatever you do will turn out right" (Proverbs 4:26, GNT).

- "Work hard at whatever you do" (Ecclesiastes 9:10, GNT).

- "Do faithfully whatever you do" (3 John 5).

- "And whatever you do, do it heartily, as to the Lord and not to men" (Colossians 3:23).

- "Remember that God is going to judge you for whatever you do" (Ecclesiastes 11:9, GNT).

- "Therefore, whether you eat or drink, or whatever you do, do all to the glory of God" (1 Corinthians 10:31).

In Colossians 3:17, the phrase "word or deed," is just a way of saying all our activities in the world. The words we speak should be as though Jesus were speaking them. The things we do should be as though Jesus were doing them.

Laura Duvall gives us a picture of what this means: "When my daughter Aimee was in nursery school, she'd come home each day with drawings, collages, and other projects. Next to her own name she'd scrawl the name of someone she loved— usually Mommy or Daddy, sometimes baby brother Ben. 'I did this for you,' she'd proudly write. If Aimee could do every school project for me or for her dad, surely I can do my 'projects' for my heavenly Father. Now I often ask myself, '*Have I written my Lord's name on all I have done today?*'"[22]

"Whatever we do in the name of Christ ought to be joined with thanksgiving. If we cannot give thanks, then we had better not do it or say it! This is the fifth of six references in Colossians to thanksgiving (Col. 1:3, 12; 2:7; 3:15, 17; 4:2). When we remember that Paul was a Roman prisoner when he wrote this letter, it makes this emphasis on thanksgiving that much more wonderful."[23]

In this powerful section of his letter to the Colossians, Paul told us to …

- Let the peace of Christ arbitrate.

- Let the word of Christ permeate.

- Let the name of Christ motivate.

"In the fable *The Emperor's New Clothes*, an unscrupulous con artist, seeking royal favor, promised to provide the emperor with an outfit of clothing that would be very special. In fact, so delicate and rare would be the fabric that the clothes would be undetectable to the touch. And more importantly, these new clothes would be invisible to anyone of poor character or inferior ability.

"When the emperor received the empty hanger on which his new outfit was supposedly displayed, he could hardly admit to not seeing the clothes without impugning his own suitability for royal office. So he admired the clothes (as did his advisors), put them on, and strutted proudly around his kingdom—stark naked!

"If we're not careful, we Christians can fall into the same trap. We can obediently take off the clothes of the old life, (such as lying, greed, and sexual impurity). But if we fail to replace those old garments with the new robes of righteousness presented in this chapter, we'll parade around acting as if we have put them on when in reality we're spiritually naked. And just as in the case of the emperor, the world will snicker behind our backs because they see us as we really are and not as we are pretending to be."[24]

Don't fail to receive the grace of Christ, put on the character of Christ, submit to the peace of Christ, dwell on the Word of Christ, and live for the name of Christ.

The well-dressed believer is the one who is clothed in hand-me-downs from the closet of the Carpenter of Nazareth.

CHAPTER 8

The Christian Household

COLOSSIANS 3:18 – 4:1

THE STORY IS TOLD OF A WOMAN WHO WAS BROWSING in a Christian bookstore one day when she discovered a shelf of reduced items. Among them, was a figurine of a man and a woman, their heads lovingly tilted toward one another. On the bottom was the inscription: "Happy 10th Anniversary." It appeared to be in perfect condition, yet the tag on the figurine said, "DAMAGED."

When the woman turned the tag over, she read this explanation: "Wife is coming unglued."

That tag could describe many modern marriages, couldn't it? Wives and husbands are coming unglued, and homelife is in crisis in America and around the world. The rate of people getting married in America is at its lowest point since the U.S. government began keeping records in 1867. When I was born, approximately eighty percent of U.S. households were made up of married couples. Now that number is under fifty percent.

Attitudes about marriage have changed dramatically just in the past few years. As recently as 2006, about half of U.S. adults said it was very important for couples having children to legally marry. By 2020, that number had fallen to 29 percent. The publication, *The Hill*, which reported these results, said, "The institution of marriage in America appears to have become increasingly inconsequential for growing numbers of young men and women, including couples having children together."[1]

It's not just marriages and homes that are frayed. Despite the largest global population in history, there's never been more loneliness, polarization, and acrimony on every side. Look in any direction you want—personally, politically, globally—and the world is bathed in bad blood.

Frankly, I'd be discouraged were it not for Colossians 3 and the biblical teachings here by Paul the apostle. There's no passage in Paul's writing more relevant to our daily relationships than what he says in this extended paragraph that begins in Colossians 3:18 and runs through the first verse of chapter 4.

He is very succinct here, and reading his words is no chore. As you'll see, Paul deals with three vital relationships. For those who have now come to live "in Christ," he outlines the responsibilities of husbands and wives, parents and children, and masters and servants.

Take time to soak in these words:

Wives, submit yourselves to your husbands, as is
fitting in the Lord. Husbands, love your wives and do

not be harsh with them. Children, obey your parents in everything, for this pleases the Lord. Fathers, do not embitter your children, or they will become discouraged.

Slaves, obey your earthly masters in everything; and do it, not only when their eye is on you and to curry their favor, but with sincerity of heart and reverence for the Lord. Whatever you do, work at it with all your heart, as working for the Lord, not for human masters, since you know that you will receive an inheritance from the Lord as a reward. It is the Lord Christ you are serving. Anyone who does wrong will be repaid for their wrongs, and there is no favoritism.

Masters, provide your slaves with what is right and fair, because you know that you also have a Master in heaven (Colossians 3:18–4:1, NIV).

Instruction to Wives

Paul began with a word to wives, and this is among the most disputed and controversial of all Paul's writings, so we need to deal with it biblically and accurately. Let's not run away from this teaching, but let's make sure we understand it in the full context of Scripture. It's a wonderful word of advice if we do that, a truth to be embraced.

Paul said: "Wives, submit to your own husbands, as is fitting in the Lord" (Colossians 3:18).

In early times, this phraseology was included in marriage ceremonies, but no longer. I can almost imagine hearing a gasp from the audience if this phrase were still spoken. Modern brides and grooms don't want it in their vows, even though it's right here in the Bible.

In Paul's day, as well as in ours, the concept of submission was very negative. Culturally, submission conveyed the idea of weakness. A person didn't submit because in doing so they would convey the idea they were weak or subservient. Whether they were submitting to someone who was governing them or to authorities, to submit was interpreted as weakness of character, and it implied humiliation.

From a scriptural perspective, much of the resistance, confusion, and fear about this word and its truth is the result of incomplete biblical research and careless interpretation. Three realities about submission are often left out of the discussion, and I want to share them with you so we don't lose this precious ingredient in our relationships.

The Concept of Submission

The books of Colossians and Ephesians seem to have been written at about the same time. Scholars believe Paul wrote Ephesians, which he then used as a rough model for penning his special letter to the Colossians. You'll notice many parallels between these two books, including Paul's counsel on marriage. In the Ephesians passage, Paul tells us to be filled with the Spirit. The evidence of the Spirit's control and empowerment of our lives will be threefold: We'll speak to each other in psalms, hymns, and spiritual songs; we'll give thanks without ceasing to God; and we'll submit to one another in the fear of God (Ephesians 5:18-21).

Notice that third evidence of being filled with the Spirit. Ephesians 5:21 says: "Submitting to one another in the fear of God." As we continue reading in Ephesians, we discover Paul applied that principle to the same relationships we see in Colossians—to marriage, to parents and children, and to slaves and masters. In all these relationships, there needs to be a spirit of submission. This is mutual submission! If you think that God is picking on women in this passage, He is not!

Michael J. Kruger says,

The ultimate demonstration that submission is a good and biblical virtue is that it was practiced by our Lord himself. Christ, in his earthly ministry, submitted himself to the Father (John 4:34; 5:3). His submission was so complete that he was "obedient to the point of death, even death on a cross" (Phil. 2:8).

Here's the point: submission is not a female virtue; it's a Christian virtue .... When we as Christians—both male and female—deny ourselves and submit ourselves to those in authority over us, we are doing something distinctively Christlike. Whenever we say, "Not as I will, but as you will," we are acting like Jesus.[2]

The Center of Submission

Let's go even deeper. Our submission isn't so much to another human or human institution—it's to the Lord Himself. James 4:7 says, "Therefore submit to God."

You'll see this in Ephesians and Colossians, too, if you look carefully. Ephesians 5:22 says, "Wives, submit to your own husbands, as to the Lord." And Colossians 3:18 says, "Wives, submit to your own husbands, as is fitting in the Lord."

In other words, our true submission is to the Lord—to His will and to His Lordship.

Where has our Christian vocabulary gone? We once talked about surrendering to Christ, yielding everything to Him, and submitting to His will alone. We sang hymns that said, "Have thine own way, Lord" and "I surrender all." We talked of total commitment, of nailing our colors to the mast, and of denying ourselves, taking up our cross, and following Him. Thankfully, this theme isn't totally lost to today's sermons, books, music, and appeals. But we must never underestimate its importance.

The demands of Calvary haven't changed, but our culture has. We've never been more self-assertive, egocentric, and personally defensive of our rights. We're not keen to submit to others because we've forgotten about submitting to Christ Jesus in all areas, at all times.

Elisabeth Elliot was one of the great Christian women of the twentieth century. She was often asked about this passage, and she quoted Oswald Chambers, who said, "Submission means surrender to another, but in the evangelical sense it means that I conduct myself actually among men as the submissive child of my Father in heaven."

Elisabeth went on to say, "Let's look first at the Son of God, perfect in His submission to His Father. His whole life on earth demonstrated an unconditional surrender to that glorious will .... Do we want to follow Him in this?"

Yes, she said, but too many people look for loopholes.[3]

Don't look for loopholes. Let's surrender ourselves without reservation to Jesus Christ and be humble as we navigate all our relationships. Let's be submissive to one another. The primary relationship in a wife's life is not her relationship to her husband. Her primary relationship is her relationship with the Lord. The priorities of a godly wife are the Lord first, her husband second, her children third, and her other responsibilities after that. Obedience at the first level will insure obedience at the remaining levels.

The Context of Submission

We must also understand the context of submission. Look again at Colossians 3:18. It says, "Wives, submit to your own husbands."

It does *not* say all women are to be submissive to all men. This submission concept applies here only to marriage. Paul made it clear to the Galatians that when it comes to our relationship with Christ, we all stand on the same level: "For as many of you as were baptized into Christ have put on Christ. There is neither Jew nor Greek, there is neither slave nor free, there is neither male nor female; for you are all one in Christ Jesus" (Galatians 3:27-28).

Writer Edie Wadsworth warns that marriage can be difficult. "The part you're not ready for is the fact that marriage is by far the most daunting thing you'll ever do. Nobody tells you how much sacrifice and forgiveness and dying to yourself there will be. Nobody warns you that the feelings will come and go .... And nobody tells you that all of that is normal."

One of the secrets of her marriage, Edie said, is the moment when she and her husband, Stevie, observe the Lord's Supper at their church. "We walk together and kneel at the communion rail, holding out our hands like beggars .... We begin to submit to the sanctifying—dare I say crucifying—work of Christ in our hearts."

"Jesus is the skillful potter," wrote Edie, "chipping away at our rough edges—our bitterness and hardheartedness and self-righteousness and sin." And she added this vital secret: "Peace in my marriage finally came when I quit looking for peace with my husband and started looking for peace with God."[4]

Instruction to Husbands

Since wives are asked to submit to their husbands, we might expect that husbands would be challenged to rule or lead their wives. But the apostle Paul does not say that. Instead, he instructs husbands to love their wives.

"Husbands, love your wives and do not be bitter toward them" (Colossians 3:19).

Paul begins his instruction to husbands by urging them not to act harshly toward their wives. He forbids bitter and sharp behavior. Instead, husbands are to love their wives with a Christlike heart of love.

The word Paul uses here for "love" is the word *agape*. It's "the distinctly Christian word for the kind of sacrificial, self-giving love whose model is Christ himself."[5] We must love with the sacrificial love of Christ.

Husbands Are to Love Their Wives Unconditionally

Since we've already introduced the passage in Ephesians, we should consider it a cross-reference that helps us expand our understanding of what the Lord intends. In the Ephesians parallel passage, Paul added these remarkable words: "Husbands, love your wives, just as Christ also loved the church" (Ephesians 5:25).

This is almost too deep to grasp. Christ loved the Church by giving her everything He was and everything He had. He left the realms of eternal glory, descended to earth, lived in poverty, and ultimately gave His life for His Church. He suffered as none has ever suffered, and He loved as none has ever loved.

And that's the way I'm supposed to love my wife?

Yes.

And, oh, the Church is so imperfect. Christ was under no illusion when He sought us in love. Did He know that after He died on the cross for us we would fail Him many times? Yes, He did. He is omniscient. But He loved us in spite of all of that. He loved us as we were and as He knew we would be. He loved us with our flaws. There was nothing in us that caused Him to love us. He didn't love us on the basis of our performance.

He loved us with a never-ending, self-sacrificial focus. He still does and always will, despite our halting progress through life.

Our love in marriage must embrace all of the faults and failures that we each bring to the relationship. Christ's love for us was not idealized; it was not romanticized. He loved us as we are, and a husband must love his wife as she is.

I don't know about you, but during the pandemic I heard a number of heart-stirring stories of couples like Larry and Sue Loring of Fresno, California. They had been married for decades and were dedicated to their local church and to their ministry of foster parenting. But Larry developed non-Hodgkin's lymphoma, while Sue was diagnosed with Alzheimer's. The two took care of each other as best they could, loving each other unconditionally through all their stress. Sue passed away, and ten days later Larry followed her to heaven. One of their adopted grandchildren said, "He fought so hard to hold on for so long .... He was in a lot of pain. I feel like once he knew Grammy was OK and she wasn't suffering ... he finally felt he could go."[6]

In the past few years, it's amazing how many elderly couples died within days or hours of one another. They were driving themselves to stay alive in order to care for the other; and when that obligation ceased, they, too, were ready to go. There's longevity in unconditional love. In fact, it's eternal. The Bible says, "Love never ends" (1 Corinthians 13:8, CSB).

Husbands Are to Love Their Wives Sacrificially

"Husbands, love your wives, just as Christ also loved the church and gave Himself for her" (Ephesians 5:25).

The supreme demonstration of the costliness of love is seen in what Jesus Christ did when He went to the cross. Love is expensive. Just as Christ gave Himself up on behalf of

His Bride, the Church, so the husband is to give himself up sacrificially for the benefit of his wife.

Husbands and wives know what it's like to give up some of the things on their priority list so they can serve each other. Love means sacrifice. When you love someone, you are willing to give for them, and give up for them, and yes, even give in for them because you care about their needs more than you care about your own.

Zoanne Wilkie was a popular speaker at women's events. One morning, she said, she was upset that her husband, David, never gave her any flowers. The thought worsened when she turned on the radio and heard the Barbra Streisand and Neil Diamond song that says, "You don't bring me flowers anymore .... You don't sing me love songs."

She bundled up and went into the garage to get into the old Chrysler. It was a cold day, and she dreaded getting the car started. But she realized it had already been warmed up for her. David had made sure it was warm when she got into it. She said, "Thank you for the flowers."

Later that week, she had to put something in the garbage compactor, and she dreaded opening it because she knew it was overflowing. But David had emptied it and put in a new bag. She said, "Thank you for the flowers."

Shortly afterward, Zoanne was feeling ill, but she dreaded going to the doctor. "He'll tell me to lose weight," Zoanne complained to David. He said, "I'll go with you."

"I don't want you to hear him tell me to lose weight," she said.

David tilted his head and said, "What's the difference if you weigh one pound per cubic inch, or three pounds per cubic inch? I'm absolutely crazy about you!"

Zoanne said, "Oh, David! Three dozen, long stemmed, American Beauty Roses!"

On another occasion, Zoanne was speaking at a women's weekend retreat an hour's drive from home. She didn't think her presentation was going well. All the women looked like faces chiseled on Mount Rushmore. Late that evening, she called David.

"Hello," he said, sounding sleepy.

"Honey, I hate to bother you at this time of the night .... It's just that I'm having a really hard time with this group. Would you please pray for me?"

David prayed a rather sleepy prayer for her, and she hung up and went to bed. An hour later, there was a knock at the door. There stood David, standing in the rain. "I thought you needed a buddy," he said. To Zoanne it was like a spring bouquet.[7]

No spouse is perfect, and we all fail in many ways. But sacrificial love never fails. How can you more faithfully practice it in your relationships? Do you know someone who needs a bunch of flowers?

Husbands Are to Love Their Wives Purposefully

There's a God-ordained purpose to it all. Love isn't a cloud that floats around in the air at the whim of the winds. It's a beam of sunshine that aims to give light and heat. Going back to Ephesians 5, Paul said, "That He might sanctify and cleanse her with the washing of water by the word, that He might present her to Himself a glorious church, not having spot or wrinkle or any such thing, but that she should be holy and without blemish" (verses 26-27).

Christ has a purpose in loving the Church. His ultimate goal is to present the Church to Himself as a glorious Church without spot or wrinkle or any such thing —a "holy and without blemish" Bride.

How does that translate into our marriages today? Listen carefully. I have a goal in loving my wife that is reflected here in this purpose clause. My prayer is that I will never be guilty of holding my wife back from being what God wants her to be out of deference to my own selfish needs. Rather, I want to edify her, build her up, and strengthen her in every way.

Husbands Are to Love Their Wives Passionately

"So husbands ought to love their own wives as their own bodies; he who loves his wife loves himself. For no one ever hated his own flesh, but nourishes and cherishes it, just as the Lord does the church" (Ephesians 5:28-29).

The Bible says we're to love our wife the same way we love ourselves. That is a superfluous statement because the Scripture says that in marriage we become one flesh. So, I don't love my wife as myself. I love my wife because she is myself. And I am herself. We are one.

Here are two special actions that will help husbands love their wives.

We Are to Nourish Our Wives

When a husband nourishes his wife, he sees that her needs are met. It ought to be a fulfilling task for the husband to do everything he can to meet his wife's needs.

Nourish is a picture of investing in our wives with a view to her well-being. This is what it means to provide emotional nutrition for our wives. Here are some nourishing words that we cannot forget about.

- "I do not feel complete without you."

- "I appreciate the way you have cared for me all these years. I'm glad I married you."

- "It's nice to wake up next to you."

- "I'm proud of you."

- "I love you."

- "I'll go to the mall with you."

We Are to Cherish Our Wives

The word "cherish" is used in the New Testament to describe a nurse caring for a sick patient or a mother caring for a newborn baby. And what's at the core of cherishing is one word that isn't in the vocabulary of too many husbands: it's the word *tenderness*.

Those whose spouses have preceded them to heaven often look back and realize how they underestimated the importance of the little things—a quiet dinner on the patio, a Friday night at the local high school football game, the joint task of washing and drying the dishes. At the time, these things seemed so regular and routine that little emotional value was attached to them. But later, one realizes those shared moments were more precious than they realized.

Let's cherish one another and appreciate the little moments.

Instruction to Children

In Colossians 3:20, Paul turns his attention to the children in the Church. Perhaps you've been in a church service in which the pastor addresses the youngsters. Sometimes all the children come to the front of the room for a children's sermon.

To Paul, the children were as important as any other group, so in verse 20 he said, "Children, obey your parents in all things, for this is well pleasing to the Lord."

The one thing he wanted children to understand was obedience. That is a fundamental building block of the home and, indeed, of all life. Whether there are Christians in that home or not, obedience is what makes a family work.

If we look at this verse carefully and at its parallel passage in Ephesians 6, we'll find four biblical reasons for obeying your parents.

Obedience Is a Principle of Morality

First, obedience is a principle of morality and righteousness. Colossians 3:20 says, "Children, obey your parents in all things, for this is well pleasing to the Lord." Ephesians 6:1 adds, "For this is right."

How plain and simple is this truth. There is an order in nature, ordained by God, and it argues for the rightness of certain actions, and it is right that a child should obey his parents.

Obedience Is a Precept of Scripture

Second, obedience is a vital biblical practice, one we should learn as early as possible. Ephesians 6:2 says, "'Honor your father and mother,' which is the first commandment with promise."

In the list of Ten Commandments in Exodus 20, God listed the first four with no special promise attached to any of them. But when we get to this fifth commandment something changes: "Honor your father and your mother, that your days may be long upon the land which the Lord your God is giving you" (verse 12). Why the promise? I believe that God was underlining the great importance of this instruction. We're to obey our parents because this is God's design, which, if violated, could well shorten our lives.

People magazine reported on an eight-year-old Ohio boy who took his four-year-old sister on a joy ride to McDonalds after they began craving cheeseburgers. It happened on a Sunday night after the children's father had fallen asleep. The eight-year-old grabbed his piggy bank, got the van keys, strapped his little sister in the back, and drove one mile to the local McDonalds. He pulled into the drive-in window. At first, the employees thought it was a joke, but when they saw there were no adults in the vehicle, they called the police.

Here's the surprising thing. The boy drove perfectly, through four intersections and over a set of railroad tracks. He didn't hit a single thing, and he kept to the speed limit. He obeyed all the laws perfectly. When the police asked him how he had learned to drive, he told them it was by watching YouTube videos. But the boy broke down in tears when he realized how reckless he'd been, and he was contrite when his parents picked him and his sister up at the station.[8]

I'm glad that boy learned to obey all the traffic laws! I'm sure the parents learned a lesson too. The story could have turned out tragically. Children shouldn't have to learn obedience on YouTube videos. When we open God's Word and teach them how to navigate life with faith and obedience, it can keep their lives safe. There's all kinds of parental neglect happening in our land today, but we cannot afford to let our children learn their values from a screen. For their own protection, they need us to help them learn the joy of obedience.

Obedience Is a Protection for Children

That brings us to the next benefit of obedience. In the Ephesians 6 passage, Paul uses three entire verses to tell children to obey, and he intends it as a protection to them: "Children, obey your parents in the Lord, for this is right. 'Honor your father and mother,' which is the first commandment with promise: 'that it may be well with you and you may live long on the earth'" (verses 1-3).

There may be disobedient rebels out there who have violated this command and have somehow made it through life unscathed, but I've honestly never met one. Everybody has to report to somebody. That doesn't stop when a person turns twenty. Everyone needs to learn the principle of submission to authority. If we don't learn it at home where it is supposed to be learned, we'll struggle with it all of our lives. And someday there will be a notation in our employee file that says, "Struggles with authority."

Obedience Is a Prerequisite for a Long Life

"That ... you may live long on the earth" (Ephesians 6:3).

Discipline in a child's life is usually conducive to good health. Does that mean that a person who is disobedient always dies young and a person who is obedient always lives into his nineties? No, of course not! Nevertheless, we know from common sense this is a general truth in life. A person who grows up in rebellion against authority has put himself on a path that leads to discouragement and destruction. People who follow God's instructions have a much better chance of living a longer life.

Instruction to Parents

As we continue reading Colossians 3, we have a verse just for parents: "Fathers, do not provoke your children, lest they become discouraged" (Colossians 3:21). The parallel text in Ephesians says, "And you, fathers, do not provoke your children to wrath, but bring them up in the training and admonition of the Lord" (Ephesians 6:4). Parenting can exasperate us, but we're not to exasperate our kids. Instead, we're to train and admonish them in the ways of our Lord Jesus Christ.

Don't irritate your children or discourage them by unreasonable demands or condescending neglect. Some parents are always on their kids' backs, harping at them, snapping at them. In fairness, every parent struggles with the momentary pressures of child-raising, but Paul is talking about an ongoing attitude. Our children will absorb our emotions and attitudes, and we want to make sure they absorb the best ones possible.

Before he deployed to Afghanistan a few years ago, Army Staff Sgt. Philip Gray sat down and wrote 270 messages for his seven-year-old daughter—one for each day he would be away. Some of his notes for Rosie encouraged her to do her best at school and excel in her activities and hobbies. Others included doodles like snowmen or pumpkins to represent holidays missed. And each morning he was gone, his wife, Kristen, would slip a new note into Rosie's lunch box just so she would know how much he loved her. Philip returned three days before Rosie's eighth birthday, and can you guess what she requested? "Daddy, can you keep writing me those notes?"[9]

Rather than discouraging our children, we as parents are instructed to "bring them up" (Ephesians 6:4). To bring up children is a scriptural phrase that implies a serious responsibility for their spiritual, moral, mental, and physical well-being.

Paul concludes that this "bringing up" is to be done "in the training and admonition of the Lord" (Ephesians 6:4).

Training is correction. Admonition is instruction or teaching. We need to teach our kids. We are responsible to help them learn the difference between right and wrong. We are to help them learn the Scriptures and motivate them to follow what they learn.

Instruction to Employees

Next, Paul turns to the relationships between bond-servants and masters, saying, "Bondservants, obey in all things your masters according to the flesh, not with eyeservice, as men-pleasers, but in sincerity of heart, fearing God" (Colossians 3:22).

The word "bondservants" means "slaves." This instruction was given in the days when Rome ruled most of the world. There were millions of slaves across the empire. The vast majority of businesses in New Testament times were family operated, and almost all of the work force could be summarized under the heading of slaves or servants. By addressing these people, Paul is not endorsing slavery but rather speaking into a situation that existed for many years.

The slaves were the farmers, the sanitation people, the educators, the nannies, the shop keepers. Paul knew that many of these slaves were coming to faith in Jesus Christ. All across the empire, Christian slaves would be experiencing every kind of treatment at the hands of every sort of master.

Some masters were undoubtedly cruel and heartless; others would be kind, treating their servants like family. Some of their masters would be brother Christians; others would be pagans. Some would be hostile to the faith. Paul's words here embrace all of these situations as well as the situations we're in today, such as the relationships between employer and employee.

The instructions we're coming to as we leave Colossians 3 and enter chapter 4 are for anyone who lives within the authority structure of the marketplace. How should we function? How should we live? How should we work? In Paul's opinion, Christianity is meant to work in the stress and strain of the real world, in the grit and grind of the marketplace.

The Employee's Action

He begins with this instruction: "Bondservants, obey in all things your masters" (Colossians 3:22).

The Bible clearly tells us that how we work—our actions—are a witness to those who watch us. This was a common theme for Paul. In his letter to Titus, he wrote, "Exhort bondservants to be obedient to their own masters, to be well pleasing in all things, not answering back, not pilfering, but showing all good fidelity, that they may adorn the doctrine of God our Savior in all things" (2:9-10).

Think of it this way—the way you work for your employer can change the opinion people have of Christ.

The Employee's Assignment

Our assignment in the workforce is to faithfully fulfill our duties to the men or women God has placed in authority over us, whether they are Christians or not.

Sometimes Christian employees think that because their employer is a believer, they can be cavalier in their attitude toward work because they know the boss won't get in their face. Listen to what the Word of God has to say about that: "And those who have believing masters, let them not despise them because they are brethren, but rather serve them because those who are benefited are believers and beloved" (1 Timothy 6:2).

Larry Peabody suggests that secular work is full-time ministry service. While some people view "the ministry" as being paid by a Christian organization, Peabody reminds us we're all ministers wherever we are. Those who work in a factory, school, company, establishment, or store are truly on the front lines of Kingdom work. "In the New Testament," wrote Peabody, "God does not depict the Christian life as divided into sacred and secular parts. Rather, He shows it as a unified life, one of wholeness, in which we may single-mindedly serve Him even in our everyday work."[10]

Think of it this way. If we were all in so-called "full-time" or "vocational" ministry, there would never be enough financial income for everyone's salaries. But when you work for, say, Walmart, the company pays you to be a minister in its stores. If you work for Ford, the company pays to have your Christian presence in its factories, garages, or showrooms. If you work for American Express, someone else is giving you a salary, benefits, and an arena in which you can represent Christ by attitude, deed, and often words.

The Employee's Attitude

That means we cannot squander our ministry by going to work each day with a bad attitude. Colossians 3:22-23 says, "Not with eyeservice, as men-pleasers, but in sincerity of heart, fearing God. And whatever you do, do it heartily, as to the Lord and not to men."

Jacob Ogle was profiled in his hometown newspaper as being one of forty outstanding business leaders under the age of forty in Knoxville, Tennessee. He's involved in real estate development. The reporter asked him, "What is your biggest professional goal?"

Jacob answered, "Colossians 3:23-24 and to avoid bankruptcy."[11]

That's a good answer, and it's in the right order! In fact, the first goal will maximize the possibility of the second. When we carry a positive, biblical attitude to work every day, we're much more likely to succeed at whatever we're doing.

"Eyeservice" refers to performing tasks only superficially and doing only what can be seen—"going through the motions" of service. It may also refer to doing something only to catch the master's eye, that is, to please those in authority. Or it may refer to working only when one is being watched.[12]

Martyred missionary Jim Elliot once made this statement: "Wherever you are, *be all there*. Live to the hilt every situation you believe to be the will of God."[13]

I've chosen Colossians 3:23 as my life verse. I have preached on it several times, but I want you to see it in the context in which it appears in the Bible. It simply describes how to go about living the Christian life.

The Employee's Award

Here's a final thing to remember. When we work heartily as unto the Lord, our compensation is far more than a paycheck. Colossians 3:24-25 says, "Knowing that from the Lord you will receive the reward of the inheritance; for you serve the Lord

Christ. But he who does wrong will be repaid for what he has done, and there is no partiality."

When we work hard and no one seems to notice, we can become discouraged and forget we're not working for a boss we can see, but for the One whom we cannot see but who sees all we do. This unseen Boss will one day give out the rewards for service.

Instruction to Employers

As we turn to Colossians 4:1, we see Paul's focus turn to employers, and we can sum up his counsel in one word: Humility.

Respect Your Employees

He begins by saying, "Masters, give your bondservants what is just and fair" (Colossians 4:1). We must treat those who answer to us justly and fairly. One author described it this way:

On a day to day basis, the good leader is one who will listen to you, stand up for you, trust you and not micromanage every aspect of your work. They communicate clearly, constantly, and in a collaborative manner. They seek your advice, listen to your concerns, and consult you on the best solutions for success. They set high expectations and encourage you to be the best you can be ... striving for new heights of excellence. They also care about your life outside of work and want you to have good physical, social, and mental health. Lastly, the good boss can be tough when needed. They live in reality and know there are some who will not respond to their leadership, and, may be required to use their authority to reprimand and/or terminate staff.

However, this is always a last recourse after all other positive strategies have failed. Overall, I see the good boss as one who lives sacrificially for the benefit of others, always desiring their success as well as the success of the agency.[14]

Remember That You Also Have a Master

Respecting our workers or employees will come naturally if we remember that we ourselves are under authority, and our ultimate authority is Christ Himself. Colossians 4:1 continues, "Knowing that you also have a Master in heaven."

Whatever authority we may have is from God, and to this God both we and our workers report. Before God a boss is no more worthy than his or her workers, since God does not show partiality.

We've covered a lot of territory, but it's all about staying healthy in all the relationships the Lord ordains for us. The third chapter of Colossians begins by reminding us we're to set our affections on things above and not things on this earth. The chapter ends by again challenging us to keep our eyes on Christ. Wives are instructed to be subject to their own husbands as is fitting in the Lord. Husbands are told to love their wives as Christ loves the Church. Children are told to obey their parents in all things because this is well-pleasing to the Lord. Employees are told to obey their employers, for in doing so, they serve the Lord Jesus Christ. And employers are reminded that they also have a Master in heaven.

Christ changes everything.

Let me close this chapter by telling you about a science project that many parents have tried with their children. Take two glasses of water—a glass of cold water and a glass of warm water. Add a drop or even a capful of food coloring to each glass. In both cases the coloring will eventually diffuse throughout the glass, but it happens much more quickly in the warm water. The water molecules have more energy and move faster than in the cold water, which makes it easier for the dye to permeate the entire glass.

For those who know Christ, God has poured an abundance of grace into our hearts. If our hearts tend to be cold, that grace doesn't pervade our relationships very quickly. But if we're fervent about serving the Lord, all our relationships will be tinted with grace, "because the love of God has been poured out in our hearts by the Holy Spirit who was given to us" (Romans 5:5).

CHAPTER 9

Christian Communication

COLOSSIANS 4:2-6

GUY KAWASAKI CALLS HIMSELF A SECULAR EVANGELIST. He took the biblical word *evangelist* and transferred it to concepts such as marketing as he helped popularize the Macintosh computer in the early 1980s. Today he's an author, speaker, and consultant in business and marketing circles. He's also a storyteller.

One of his stories involves Karen Muller, who served in the Peace Corps in the late 1980s, digging wells and helping to build schools in a small village in the Philippines. One night, a group from the New People's Army, the armed wing of the Communist Party of the Philippines, came to her hut to question her about her work.

Thankfully, the villagers had warned her earlier in the day that this was going to happen, so Karen had the time to create a strategy to deal with the soldiers. She collected sugar and coffee, and when the NPA arrived, she welcomed them, saying, "Thank God you're here. I've been waiting all day. Please have some coffee. Leave your guns at the door." The leader of the group was baffled, but he put down his gun and sat down for a cup of coffee. Over coffee, they made conversation and kept a friendly tone. At the end of the coffee, the group left.

Later Karen explained her strategy, saying, "You can't interrogate someone you're having coffee with."

As Kawasaki told that story, he pointed out that Karen Muller shifted the situation from intimidation to conversation and communication. She delighted the leader of the group with unexpected hospitality and coveted coffee. That changed his heart, his mind, and his actions.

The word Kawasaki used for this was *enchantment*.

"She enchanted him," wrote Kawasaki. "Enchantment can occur in villages, stores, dealerships, offices, boardrooms, and on the Internet .... [It] transforms situations and relationships. It converts hostility into civility .... It changes skeptics and cynics into believers."[1]

Kawasaki calls it "enchantment," but it's close to what the Bible calls "evangelism"—winning people over with the good news of Jesus Christ.

A cup of coffee, a kind word, a moment of concern, an offered prayer, a quoted verse, a sincere compliment, a warm smile—these simple things can attract others, reduce conflicts, spread goodwill, and lead many to know Christ as Savior.

Dr. Sam Chan wrote:

The pattern in the New Testament seems to be this: Someone meets Jesus and experiences reconciliation with God. There is an outpouring of joy, which is often expressed through a meal with Jesus. But it's usually not a small, one-on-one meal with him. It's a banquet where the person opens his home and invites many friends to come along to meet and to eat with Jesus. The joy that comes from knowing Jesus is infectious. The gladness that comes from reconciliation with God has a snowballing effect ....

Christ's love for us is infectious. We want everyone to experience what we've discovered. Once we've tasted the joy of being in harmony, peace, and union with God our Creator, we want everyone else to be reconciled to God as well.[2]

That's what Paul wanted too. He had experienced the joy of reconciliation with God and couldn't stop telling everyone around him about it. He wanted to show the world how wonderful, how attractive, and how captivating Christ is.

That's why he wrote the book of Colossians. He wanted to attract the Colossian believers—and us—to the glory, beauty, and sufficiency of Jesus Christ.

Before going further, then, let's debrief what we've learned so far in Paul's epistle to the Colossians.

In the first three chapters, Paul focused his message on believers—on members of the church at Colossae. He clarified and exalted the doctrine of Christ and told them how to look to Christ, to live with Christ, and to build healthy relationships in Christ.

Now as we're coming to chapter 4, Paul turns his attention from inside the church to those who are outside. Paul was an evangelist who wanted his churches to be magnetic. He wanted believers to share their faith and lead others to the hope of Jesus Christ. He believed *in* his message, and he *believed* his message. He knew it would meet the innermost needs of those who heard it, if only they would listen.

It all starts with prayer.

How to Pray for "Outsiders"

How do we talk to God about other people? One of Paul's classic passages on prayer is Colossians 4:2-4: "Continue earnestly in prayer, being vigilant in it with thanksgiving; meanwhile praying also for us, that God would open to us a door for the word, to speak the mystery of Christ, for which I am also in chains, that I may make it manifest, as I ought to speak."

Here Paul described how we can pray personally for others.

Pray Personally

John Stonestreet, president of the Colson Center for Christian Worldview, wrote about a ninth-grade assignment he dreaded as a youngster. The boys senior high Bible class was sent out in twos to visit elderly "shut-ins." John was paired with his friend Brian, and neither relished the assignment. The first house on their list belonged to Ms. Buckner, an 89-year-old widow who lived down a rural Virginia road. They knocked on the door, and Ms. Buckner let them in. It was an awkward few minutes. No one knew what to talk about. Finally Ms. Buckner said, "Let's sing Christmas carols together."

That didn't go so well either.

"Well, Ms. Buckner," Brian said at length, "we'd best be on our way."

"Before you go, can we pray together?" said the elderly woman.

John and Brian both prayed, which took about 45 seconds. And then Ms. Buckner began to pray. "At that point in my life," John said, "I'd probably heard thousands of prayers. But there was something about this one. Ms. Buckner spoke to God as if she knew Him, with a confidence and humility that only comes when you're certain that Someone is listening."

Two years passed, and John couldn't get this praying woman out of his mind. One day he decided to pay her another visit. When she came to the door, John said, "You probably don't remember me, but two years ago I came here with my friend Brian."

"John," she smiled. "I prayed for you this morning."

Later John wrote, "Ms. Buckner became a close friend. She prayed for me every day for the rest of her life."[3]

That's a perfect example of what Paul was advising when he said, "Continue earnestly in prayer." This is a personal habit. We talk to a close Friend about those He brings into our lives and puts on our hearts. Sometimes we pray for people whom we've met only once. We pray over the things and the people God places on our hearts.

In a parallel text, Ephesians 6:18, Paul added, "Praying always with all prayer and supplication in the Spirit, being watchful to this end with all perseverance and supplication for all the saints."

Luke 18:1 tells us we should always pray and never lose heart or give up.

Paul wanted the Colossians to pray like that continually. He also wanted them to pray vigilantly. To be vigilant means "to be alert" or "to be awake," and it refers to an attitude of being spiritually alert. It means to notice what's going on around us, to be on the lookout for spiritual danger in our own lives and in the lives of others.

Peter used the same word when he wrote, "Be sober, be vigilant; because your adversary the devil walks about like a roaring lion, seeking whom he may devour" (1 Peter 5:8).

Paul also instructed the Colossians to pray "with thanksgiving." As we've seen throughout the letter, Colossians is a book of thanksgiving. If you read the four chapters of Colossians with a highlighter to mark the passages about thanksgiving, you'll be surprised how often this theme comes up.

Like Ms. Buckner, let's learn to intercede for others. Be on the lookout for how God is working in their lives, and then thank Him for the answers you see to your prayers. If you don't see spiritual progress in another person, don't lose heart. Just keep praying.

When we pray personally for unbelievers, we should pray continually, alertly, and thankfully for them!

Pray Purposefully

At this point, we might have expected Paul to tell the Colossians to pray for specific unbelievers in their lives. But he didn't do that. Instead, he requested prayer for himself: "Meanwhile praying also for us, that God would open to us a door for the word, to speak the mystery of Christ, for which I am also in chains, that I may make it manifest, as I ought to speak" (Colossians 4:3-4).

As the Colossians were praying earnestly, vigilantly, and gratefully for others in their lives, Paul also wanted them to pray for him. Specifically, Paul asked for two things: an open door for the Word and the ability to clearly proclaim the mystery of Christ. In other words, he prayed for connections and clarity.

Have you ever prayed for a connection? For open doors? In antiquity, just as today, that phrase is a metaphor for new opportunities. In the New Testament, it's frequently linked to evangelism. Let me show you three great examples:

- "Now when they had come and gathered the church together, they reported all that God had done with them, and that He had *opened the door* of faith to the Gentiles" (Acts 14:27, emphasis added).

- "A great and *effective door* has opened to me, and there are many adversaries" (1 Corinthians 16:9, emphasis added).

- "When I came to Troas to preach Christ's
  gospel, and *a door was opened* to me by the Lord"
  (2 Corinthians 2:12, emphasis added).

Paul's words in Colossians had a profound effect on a man named David A. Morel. He trained himself to offer this prayer continually—*Lord, open a door for me to say something about Christ.* It's not surprising he found people everywhere eager to hear what he shared.

Morel wrote "I boarded a plane some time ago and as I was walking down the aisle toward my seat, I prayed the Colossians 4:2-6 prayer." Within minutes, a young man in military uniform sat down in the seat beside him. The soldier was 24 years old. Morel looked over at him and said something to this effect, "You seem like a very mature young man." The soldier looked puzzled and said, "No, you don't know me very well."

The fellow was overwhelmed with personal problems and was hurting deeply, and he opened up about his difficulties. Morel pulled out his New Testament and showed him truths to help him cope with his problems. "That's just what I need," said the young man, drawn to the verses. Morel then shared the plan of salvation. The soldier looked at him and said, "God put you next to me, didn't He?"

Yes, in answer to the prayer of Colossians 4! It's strange how often this sort of thing happened to David Morel. But then, Colossians 4 was the prayer of his life. "By praying this way," said Morel, "we are asking God to help us present the

Gospel so the unbeliever will hear, understand, and receive the Lord Jesus Christ as Savior."[4]

In Colossians 4:3, Paul specifically requested prayer for an open door "to speak the mystery of Christ." In chapter 1, he explained the mystery of Christ as "Christ in you, the hope of glory. Him we preach, warning every man and teaching every man in all wisdom, that we may present every man perfect in Christ Jesus" (Colossians 1:27-28).

Paul didn't ask for a door to be opened just for him, but for the "word" or "the mystery of Christ." We need open doors for the Word!

Paul knew the human heart didn't need to be opened to him but to God's Word. It's the Word that does the work. It's the Word that has the power. It's the Word that creates new life: "The truth of the gospel, which has come to you, as it has also in all the world, and is bringing forth fruit, as it is also among you since the day you heard and knew the grace of God in truth" (Colossians 1:5-6).

In all my years of life and ministry, I've never stopped being amazed at the sheer power of Scripture.

After September 11, 2001, Brandon Blair enlisted in the United States Marine Corps. He served two combat tours. In August 2006, Brandon was shot by a sniper. He took the bullet to the chest, and his injury was severe. As he was lying in a hospital bed with no television and no phone, he happened to remember a small New Testament in his pocket. Pulling it out, he saw it also contained the book of Psalms. He began reading Psalm 40, and as he read, it's as though the Lord spoke to him personally. His life was changed at that moment. Today he's a pastor in Knoxville, Tennessee.[5]

I don't know who gave Brandon that little Gideon New Testament, but what a day when God opened the door of a wounded Marine to the power of His Word!

Now, let's press on to Colossians 4:3. For the first time in this book, Paul brings up the subject of his imprisonment, for he was writing this epistle while under house arrest in Rome, chained to a Roman soldier. He viewed his imprisonment as an illustration of the power of God to open doors for the Gospel even when people try to close them. Though Paul was chained, he was still delivering the Gospel.

A few years later, he wrote something similar to his friend Timothy: "I suffer trouble ... even to the point of chains; but the word of God is not chained" (2 Timothy 2:9).

How encouraging to remember that the Word of God cannot be restrained. The Gospel cannot be stopped. Even in the most difficult of circumstances, God still makes evangelistic connections and uses us to share His message.

As I'm writing this, I'm watching a difficult news story—the Russian invasion of Ukraine. As of this moment, I have no idea what will happen, but I'm very troubled. Yet even in the middle of this invasion, amazing things are happening. Pastor Benjamin Morrison and his family are in the city of Svitlovodsk, and in today's news was his account of the trauma of the near-continual air raid sirens.

"Whenever we do head to the bomb shelter, my family and I take the opportunity to share the hope of Christ with our neighbors," he wrote. "'Bomb shelter ministry' is ... not a ministry profile I thought I'd ever have. And yet, we are already seeing how fruitful it's been. Our neighbors have heard more about Christ, heard more Scripture, and been led in more prayer in the last week than most of them probably have in their lives."[6]

How much we can learn from that pastor! Never miss an opportunity to share Christ through your life, love, and lips. Ask God for connections, and take advantage of the ones He sends our way.

Even as we pray for connections, we must pray for clarity. Let's look at Colossians 4:4 again: "[Pray] that I may make [the Gospel] manifest, as I ought to speak."

"Manifest" means "to make visible" or "to make plainly recognizable." Paul didn't want to complicate or confuse the message of the Gospel. He just wanted to communicate it clearly.

Imagine! This is the apostle Paul making this prayer request! He had already written the book of Romans! How much more should we ask God to help us be clear and focused in sharing the Gospel!

Dr. Homer A. Kent, Jr. said, "Paul knew that the manner in which the gospel was presented is highly important. Perhaps he was thinking of how he would bear his witness when his case came up for trial. He was concerned that the gospel be made clear to his listeners, regardless of who they might be. Many a Roman had heard only a caricature of the Christian message. Paul's desire is that his readers at Colosse would join in prayer that God would make him effective when the door of opportunity opened."[7]

We're not responsible for how others respond to the Gospel, but we are responsible for the manner in which we communicate it. Effective and clear communication can make all the difference. Let me give you an example.

In 1949, George Roy and Elizabeth Wood, an American missionary couple serving in northwest China and Tibet, were forced to leave the area. A local leader named Pastor Mung took over the church of two hundred people. The Wood's returned to America, and by 1985 both of them had passed away without ever knowing what had happened to the church they started.

In 1988 the Wood's son, George, returned to China and met with Pastor Mung and his wife, who were now in their eighties. For 28 years the Communist government had done their best to extinguish the church. Pastor Mung wasn't allowed to preach, and he spent nine of those years in prison for his faith. It was illegal to baptize or "indoctrinate" anyone under eighteen. When the government finally allowed Pastor Mung to reopen the church in 1983 there were only thirty people in attendance.

Assuming that the church was on its last leg, George Wood asked, "Pastor Mung, how many believers do you have today?" Pastor Mung's wife brought them a cardboard roll held together by yarn. The first page was filled with writing—five columns: name, age, gender, address, occupation. There were around twenty names. George Wood continued turning over page after page with the names of the baptized. Finally he asked the Mungs, "How many believers do you have now?" He said, "One thousand five hundred baptized believers." In disbelief George Wood asked, "How did this happen?"

Pastor Mung smiled as he shared his secret for church growth. It wasn't a technique or a program. He simply said, "Oh! Jesus Christ is the same yesterday, today, and forever. And we pray a lot!"[8]

One man said, "If we're going to share the gospel, it's going to take prayer .... We have a role, but if we ever think that we can accomplish what God has given us to do without prayer, then we're delusional. How do we show and tell the gospel when many people are resistant? Pray. It always begins with prayer."[9]

Prayer is essential.

But it's not the only thing.

How to Live With "Outsiders"

As we pray for those around us who need the Lord, we must also become living witnesses by the way we conduct ourselves, by the way we treat others, and by the way we use our time. Colossians 4:5 goes on to say: "Walk in wisdom toward those who are outside, redeeming the time."

"Those who are outside" was one of the ways Paul described those who were outside of God's family. It is a phrase he borrowed from Jesus, who said, "To you it has been given to know the mystery of the kingdom of God; but to those who are outside, all things come in parables" (Mark 4:11).

Though Paul and Jesus considered believers to be "insiders," this was never intended to give a superiority complex. Instead, as Paul reminded the Colossians, it should motivate us to walk in wisdom toward the lost.

The word "walk" refers to the way we conduct our lives day by day. It's a reminder that how we live affects the credibility of the words we say. Our lives should be illustrations of the story we tell about Jesus. That takes wisdom!

At the beginning of the letter, Paul prayed for this very thing. He asked the Lord to fill the Colossians with "the knowledge of [God's] will in all wisdom and spiritual understanding; that [they might] walk worthy of the Lord, fully pleasing Him, being fruitful in every good work and increasing in the knowledge of God" (Colossians 1:9-10).

Now near the end of the letter, he circles back to the same ideas.

Years ago I heard a story I've never forgotten about Dr. Will H. Houghton. "When Dr. Houghton became pastor of the Baptist Tabernacle in Atlanta, a man in that city hired a private detective to follow Dr. Houghton and report on his conduct. After a few weeks, the detective was able to report to the man that Dr. Houghton's life matched his preaching. As a result, that man became a Christian."[10]

What if someone hired a detective to follow you to examine your consistency as a Christian!

Richard C. Halverson, the late chaplain of the United States Senate, said: "You've got the right to say anything you like. But others don't have to listen! They're under no obligation to tune you in; when they do, they can also tune you out anytime they wish. Your right to speak is guaranteed—but you must earn the right to be listened to. And that depends on your integrity. Integrity is the prerequisite to acceptance. If you expect to be paid attention to, back it up with your life. Let your walk correspond to your talk."[11]

Sheldon Vanauken wrote, "The best argument for Christianity is Christians: their joy, their certainty, their completeness. But the strongest argument against Christianity is also Christians—when they are somber and joyless, when they are narrow and repressive, then Christianity dies a thousand deaths."[12]

The apostle Peter put it this way: "I beg you as sojourners and pilgrims, abstain from fleshly lusts which war against the soul, having your conduct honorable among the Gentiles, that when they speak against you as evildoers, they may, by your good works which they observe, glorify God in the day of visitation" (1 Peter 2:11-12).

At this point in his passage, Paul brings up the subject of redeeming the time, or, literally, "buying up time." It's the picture of a businessman or investor who knows an opportunity to make money when he sees one. He quickly moves in before the opportunity is gone. A wise witness is on the alert to buy up opportunities to share Christ with lost people. Galatians 6:10 says, "As we have opportunity, let us do good to all."

We have to take advantage of the opportunities!

How to Speak to "Outsiders"

Finally, having told us how to pray for outsiders and how to live with them, Paul tells us how to speak to them: "Let your speech always be with grace, seasoned with salt, that you may know how you ought to answer each one" (Colossians 4:6).

From praying to living and finally to speaking. This progression is vital. The foundation of evangelism is continual prayer. Atop that is a Christlike life. Then we must learn to speak with grace. How often do we do it all in the reverse order? Or miss a step?

The phrase "seasoned with salt" intrigued me, and I spent some time searching out its meaning. Max Anders explained, "In Paul's day, salt was used as a preservative to keep food from spoiling. This would mean the believer's speech is to be free from corruption, wholesome. Salt was also used as an additive to give flavor to food. If this meaning lies behind the figure, then the believer's speech is to be interesting, witty, tactful, and appealing. Perhaps the best understanding of the reference to salt is that the believer's speech is to be both wholesome and appealing."[13]

Napoleon Kaufman was an NFL player who bought a big house in Seattle and was the envy of many. Yet he kept asking himself, "Is this it? This can't be it. Something's wrong with my life."

During his second year in the NFL, he was cussing and using terrible language during a practice session at training camp. One of his teammates—he didn't say whom—came up to him and said, in front of all the other players, "Hey, Napoleon, you don't really look like the type of guy that would be out here acting like this. Man, don't you know that God can use your life?"

It must have been the Holy Spirit that prompted the teammate because Kaufman went back to his hotel deeply affected. He kept hearing the words over and over: "Don't you know that God can use your life?" That evening Kaufman fell to his knees, repented of his sins, and was transformed by the grace of Jesus. He started reading his Bible, and he became a follower of Christ. Later he left football to serve the Lord in other ways, which he's still doing today.[14]

Think of that? An unknown player, prompted by the Lord, spoke with "salt" to a fellow player whose salty language was out of bounds. Something about the exchange was touched by God, and a man gave his life to Christ.

How about you? Are others bored when you begin talking about Jesus? Or do your words beam with excitement? Do they leave others wanting to know more about your Savior?

Max Lucado, wrote, "You have the power to change someone's life simply by the words that you speak .... Your words are to their soul what a vitamin is to their body. If you had food and saw someone starving, would you not share it? If you had water and saw someone dying of thirst, would you not give it? Of course you would. Then won't you do the same for their hearts? Your words are food and water. Do not withhold encouragement from the discouraged. Speak words that make people stronger. Believe in them as God has believed in you."[15]

Sinclair Ferguson describes what it means for our words to be seasoned with salt. He says: "My native land is Scotland. I have the privileged status of being a resident alien in the United States ... but people often remind me, 'You have an accent.'"

People often ask Ferguson, "You're not from around here, are you?"

"That is surely a parable of what it is possible for the people of God to become in the way we use our tongues, as by God's grace we learn to speak with a Jesus-like accent," wrote Ferguson, drawing out the lesson. "Do you speak like someone who 'sounds' a little like Jesus because ... you have found pardon and renewal in Christ, and now his Word dwells richly in you?"[16]

Finally, Paul says we are to "know how to answer everyone" (Colossians 4:6, NIV).

This reminds us of Peter's words: "Always be prepared to give an answer to everyone who asks you to give the reason for the hope that you have. But do this with gentleness and respect" (1 Peter 3:15, NIV).

Let's recap.

We need to pray for outsiders by praying personally and purposefully for connections and clarity. Take some time right now to ask God to lead you across the path of someone whom He is preparing to hear the Gospel. Pray that you'll recognize the opportunity and present Christ plainly and clearly.

We need to live with outsiders, walking before them in wisdom and redeeming the time.

And we need to speak to them with words of grace, seasoned with salt, that we may know how we ought to answer each one.

Russell E. Gehrlein had a stellar career in the Army, and he's a gifted Bible teacher and writer. In a blog post, he explained how he came to faith in Christ at age seventeen. He said that though he grew up in a church-going family, he never heard the Gospel preached in a way he could understand. In the mid-1970s, he saw some popular musical productions about Christ, and they prompted something in his heart.

The summer before his senior year in high school—June of 1975—he took part in a Boy Scout canoe trip in northern Minnesota and Canada. He started praying more—praying, for example, that he would catch fish and see wildlife.

During Russell's senior year in high school, his main goal was to take the right girl to the prom, although that proved elusive. He also wanted to become an Eagle Scout and get selected for the National Honor Society.

One day his best friend, a fellow he had known since the eighth grade, began inviting him to Youth for Christ meetings, which took place in a church across the street from the high school. Russell kept putting it off, but he finally agreed to attend the Youth for Christ Christmas party.

"I can't remember much about what we did or what the speaker said," Russell wrote. "I do recall that he explained to me for the very first time that Jesus wanted to come in and change me from the inside out. This was exactly what I needed to hear. I was doing my best to be a good boy, just like Richie Cunningham [of *Happy Days*]. However, I was only focusing on my exterior: what I did, how I looked, and what I said. I tried to be that funny, smart, popular, handsome guy everybody liked, but I always seemed to fall short."

The speaker that evening explained that Jesus wanted to live His life through us from the inside out, and he used a clarifying illustration. Imagine what would happen if a professional basketball player could somehow enter into a high school player's body. He could play the game and make the shots through the younger player.

That's what Christ wants to do.

"It made sense to me. When the speaker asked for us to bow our heads, close our eyes, and raise our hands if we wanted to follow Jesus, I did. I eagerly accepted Jesus as my Savior and Lord. I have not been the same since that day."[17]

How wonderfully God works! The inner preparation by the Spirit, the persistent invitation of a buddy, and a speaker who made the Gospel clear.

God, help us to be part of that process!

May He give us many open doors—and the courage to enter them with the Gospel!

CHAPTER 10

Paul and His Friends

COLOSSIANS 4:7-18

TWO LITTLE JEWISH GIRLS—BEST FRIENDS—GERMANY, 1939.

You're already getting the picture. Betty Grebenschikoff and Ana María Wahrenberg were nine-year-old schoolmates in Berlin. They often held hands when walking home, and their giggles and adventures mirrored their happy childhoods—until the Nazis unleashed a series of horrors against Jews on Kristallnacht. When the two girls saw each other for the last time, they hugged and wept and said goodbye in the schoolyard.

Grebenschikoff's family fled to Shanghai. Wahrenberg's family escaped to Santiago, Chile.

After the war, both girls tried to find the other. But search engines hadn't come along yet. Eventually both young ladies married, and their names changed. Decades went by, and in time both thought the other might be dead. But they never forgot about the other. "She was always on my mind," said Grebenschikoff.

One day a worker at the USC Shoah Foundation noticed similarities in the stories of the two women, whose testimonies were part of the Holocaust era. The foundation tracked down the women and arranged a reunion in Florida. Wahrenberg, accompanied by her son and his wife, flew from Chile to Florida, and Grebenschikoff came to their hotel for an emotional reunion. They are now 91 years old!

"It was like we were never separated," said Wahrenberg.

Grebenschikoff felt the same, "It was as if we had seen each other yesterday."

The women, both widowed and leaning on canes, spent four days together, laughing, shopping, eating, and talking for hours. "We're not the girls we used to be when we were 9, that's for sure, but we kept giggling like we were little kids," Grebenschikoff said.

Now they stay in touch regularly, and Grebenschikoff is planning a trip to Chile.[1]

Apart from our relationship with Christ, nothing is more enduring than our friendships. They are God's gift to us, for God knew that being alone all the time isn't good for us, not even in the Garden of Eden. That's why the second greatest command is to love one another.

The apostle Paul kept his friends as close as he could. He cherished them, leaned on them, prayed for them, and often spoke about them. There are more than one hundred different Christians (named and unnamed) associated with Paul in the book of Acts and in his epistles. In Romans 16 alone, he named 27 different friends.

For Paul, friendship was an essential part of the Christian life and Christian ministry. He was a people person, and I think that's one reason he was able to endure in life![2]

As we draw close our study of Colossians, let's notice the individuals Paul names in the final verses of his book. Remember, as far as we know, Paul had never been to the town of Colossae. Yet in our study of Colossians 4:7-18, we'll meet one ordinary person after another who influenced, befriended, and worked alongside the greatest missionary in Christian history. Without them, the apostle Paul would not have been able to carry out the ministry God gave him. To Paul, these people were indispensable, and they made his ministry possible.

I'm going to show you ten people, each one different, each one able to make a unique contribution to the common cause of the Gospel. As we go from person to person, we'll learn a lot about friendship, faithfulness, and the partnership of the Kingdom.

A Dependable Friend

Let's begin with Colossians 4:7-8: "Tychicus, a beloved brother, faithful minister, and fellow servant in the Lord, will tell you all the news about me. I am sending him to you for this very purpose, that he may know your circumstances and comfort your hearts."

Tychicus was apparently the messenger who carried the letter from Paul's prison cell in Rome to the Colossians. He also delivered the letter to the Ephesians (Ephesians 6:21). This was no easy journey. The distance between Rome and Ephesus was well over a thousand miles, and it was even further to Colossae. Travel in those days was rigorous and sometimes dangerous. If I had two original handwritten books of the New Testament to guard and deliver on a journey of over twelve hundred miles, I would hardly be able to sleep.

Paul knew he could trust Tychicus. He was a faithful friend, and he gladly entrusted him with the precious cargo.

We all need such a friend, someone who enjoys our fellowship, who loves us, and who is available to help in times of need.

When Abraham Lincoln was President, a shopkeeper named Billy Brown showed up at the White House. He had traveled from Illinois, and he said he wanted to see Mr. Lincoln. An aide asked him if he had an appointment.

"No, sir," replied Billy. 'I ain't, and it ain't necessary .... I reckon Mr. Lincoln's old friends don't need them, so you just trot along ... and tell him Billy Brown's here, and see what he says."

The aide frowned, but went. Two minutes later, the door popped open and out came Lincoln, face aglow. "Billy," he said, pumping his friend's hand, "now I am glad to see you. Come right in. You're going to stay for supper with Mary and me."

As soon as Mr. Lincoln could discharge some immediate responsibilities, the two men went to the back of the house and sat down on the stoop and, as Billy later put it, "talked and talked. He asked me about pretty nigh everybody in Springfield. I just let loose and told him about the weddings and the births and funerals and the buildings, and I guess there wasn't a yarn

I'd heard in the three and a half years he'd been away that I didn't spin for him. Laugh—you'd ought to hear him laugh—just did my heart good, for I could see what they'd been doing to him. Always was a thin man, but Lordy, he was thinner than ever now, and his face was kind of drawn and gray—enough to make you cry."

Late that evening, Billy said goodbye. The President tried to get him to stay the night, but Billy, not wanting to impose, declined. As they parted, Lincoln said, "Billy, what did you come down here for?"

"I came to see you, Mr. Lincoln."

"But you ain't asked me for anything, Billy. What is it? Out with it."

"No, Mr. Lincoln, just wanted to see you …. Been so long since I'd seen you, I was afraid I'd forget some of them yarns if I didn't unload them soon."

"Do you mean to tell me you came all the way from Springfield, Illinois, just to have a visit with me; that you ain't got no complaints in your pockets or advice up your sleeve?"

"Yes, sir. That's about it."

Tears came into Lincoln's eyes. "I'm homesick, Billy. It seems as if this war would never be over. Many a night I can see the boys dying on the fields and can hear their mothers crying for them at home, and I can't help it, Billy …. You'll never know just what good you've done me."[3]

A faithful friend does us a lot of good, and every time we see Tychicus in the New Testament, he's doing something for Paul.

Now, the question isn't if we *have* a friend like that. It's whether we *are* a friend like that. No one in the whole world is more valuable than a *Tychicus*.

A New Friend

One thing makes us feel better about Tychicus' trip to Ephesus and Colossae. He didn't travel alone. Paul sent a new friend to accompany him. Colossians 4:7-9 says, "Tychicus … will tell you all the news about me. I am sending him … with Onesimus, a faithful and beloved brother, who is one of you. They will make known to you all things which are happening here."

If the name Onesimus sounds familiar, this young man is the subject of another of Paul's letter, which was addressed to Philemon. The entire story is moving and redemptive. Onesimus was a young slave who had run away from his master, Philemon, and had somehow traveled more than twelve hundred miles to Rome. Perhaps in desperation, he sought out Paul, and the great apostle led the runaway to faith in Christ.

Onesimus was now a new friend. Though he had only recently been converted, Paul called him "a faithful and beloved brother" (verse 9).

The lesson for us? If Paul could make new friends even while under arrest, we should always be looking for new friends, for people to encourage, for souls to help. Maybe there's a neighbor or coworker you can befriend this week.

One of the most practical statements about friendship ever written came from Dale Carnegie, who said, "You can make more friends in two months by becoming interested in other people than you can in two years by trying to get other people interested in you."[4]

Long before Carnegie wrote those words, the writer of Proverbs said much the same thing: "A man who has friends must himself be friendly" (Proverbs 18:24).

That sometimes takes a bit of effort.

That's what Mary Grant Dempsey learned. She moved from the North to a Southern adult community where she knew no one and found herself very much alone. Day after day, she saw groups of cyclists riding through the community and out the gates, dressed in black Spandex riding shorts and brightly colored shirts. They appeared to be having a great time together, and Mary watched them longingly. She knew how to ride a bicycle, but she had never ridden at that level.

Shortly afterward she saw an item in the community newspaper inviting those interested in biking to join a beginners cycling group. She had to force herself to go to the organizational meeting, but she immediately met two women who chatted with her like old friends.

A dozen men and women ventured out for their first ride, pedaling slowly through the quiet streets of their community. Soon they were meeting three times a week and steadily increasing their distance. They also discovered they all enjoyed stopping frequently for refreshments, and their slogan became: "We bike for food."

Mary began attending social events, luncheons, and holiday gatherings. A small dinner group formed, and now she rides fifty to a hundred miles a week. Her health is better, and she has more friends than she ever imagined. "Taking that first step and trying something new opened up a whole new world of fun and friendship for me," she said.[5]

Television personality Andy Rooney said, "Good old friends are worth keeping whether you like them or not."

Yes, but I'd like to add that new friends are worth making—and you're almost certain to like them a lot.

A Loyal Friend

Paul next mentions a friend whose greatest trait was loyalty—Aristarchus. Colossians 4:10 says, "Aristarchus my fellow prisoner greets you." This man is named sparingly in the New Testament, but we have enough biblical references to form a composite picture. When Paul was in the final days of his extended ministry in Ephesus, a riot broke out. Thousands of people gathered in the theater (which, by the way, is still standing amid the ruins of old Ephesus). Paul wanted to address the mob, but his friends wouldn't let him.

Acts 19:29 says, "So the whole city was filled with confusion, and rushed into the theater with one accord, having seized Gaius and Aristarchus, Macedonians, Paul's travel companions."

Aristarchus survived the uproar, and when Paul left Ephesus to continue his travels, Aristarchus continued on with him (Acts 20:4). Paul continued to Jerusalem, where he triggered another riot and was arrested and sent to the Roman governor's palace in Caesarea, where he was imprisoned for two years.

When Paul was placed aboard a ship headed to Rome to stand trial before Caesar, Aristarchus was with him (Acts 27:2), and some people believe he went in the role of Paul's slave in order to gain admittance to the ship. In Rome, Paul was placed under house arrest (Acts 28), and during that time he wrote to the Colossians.

In Colossians 4:10, he wrote, "Aristarchus my fellow prisoner greets you."

"Aristarchus was a man who was always on hand when things were at their grimmest. Whenever Paul was in trouble, Aristarchus was there."[6]

When you scan the facts of that story, is there a friend in your life who would think of you as an Aristarchus? Helen Keller said, "Walking with a friend in the dark is better than walking alone in the light."

A Reconciled Friend

Now we come to a name on the list we wouldn't have expected to find, at least not by reading the book of Acts— John Mark, who also became the author of the second Gospel, the Gospel of Mark. Colossians 4:10 says, "Aristarchus my fellow prisoner greets you, with Mark the cousin of Barnabas (about whom you received instructions: if he comes to you, welcome him)."

If ever two men got started on the wrong foot, it was Paul and Mark. The whole story unfolds in Acts 13 and 14, when Paul and Barnabas are sent from Antioch as the first official church-sent missionary team in history. They went from Antioch in Syria to the island of Cyprus, where they evangelized from one end of the island to the other. With them was a relative of Barnabas, the young man named John Mark.

Paul decided he wanted to extend the journey and sail north to Asia Minor (modern-day Turkey), and that's when

Mark deserted them and returned to Antioch. We aren't given the reason, and everyone who has ever preached on the story of Mark's desertion has come up with a rich list of possibilities.

Later when Paul wanted to leave for a second missionary tour, he said to Barnabas, "Let us now go back and visit our brethren in every city where we have preached the word of the Lord, and see how they are doing" (Acts 15:38).

Barnabas agreed, but he wanted to take Mark with them again.

"But Paul insisted that they should not take with them the one who had departed from them in Pamphylia, and had not gone with them to the work" (Acts 15:39).

This quarrel broke up the first missionary team in history. Paul chose someone else and left, while Barnabas took Mark with him.

But now years had passed. Mark had proven himself, and perhaps Paul had mellowed.

William Barclay wrote, "Paul instructs the church at Colossae to receive Mark and to give him a welcome if he should come. Why does he do that? Doubtless because his churches looked with suspicion on the man whom Paul had once dismissed as useless for the service of Christ. And now Paul, with his habitual courtesy and thoughtfulness, is making sure that Mark's past will not stand in his way, by giving him full approval as one of his trusted friends. The end of Mark's career is a tribute at one and the same time to Mark and to Paul."[7]

For all of us who have failed in a ministry assignment at one time or another, John Mark is a model of encouragement.

He didn't give up or pout. He got back on his feet and back into ministry and showed himself to be a changed man, faithful to the Lord and to Paul.

And Paul, despite his strong will, warmed to Mark, forgave him if there was anything to forgive, and commended him. Later, while facing execution in Rome, Paul called for Mark because he needed him. Paul wrote to Timothy, saying, "Get Mark and bring him with you, because he is helpful to me in my ministry" (2 Timothy 4:11, NIV).

Life is too short for long resentments!

A Quiet Friend

Now we come to a mystery man in Paul's list: "Jesus, who is called Justus, also sends greetings." He went on to say that this man had "proved a comfort to me" (Colossians 4:11, NIV). We don't know anything significant about the man called Justus except for his name and the fact that he was a comfort to Paul.

Jesus would have been his Jewish name and *Justus* his Greek name. To say he was a comfort to Paul means he brought relief and consolation to him. We all need friends like Justus who can help make our sad days sunny again, who can help us move forward when we feel life giving up.

Mr. Sam Rayburn was Speaker of the United States House of Representatives longer than any other man in American history. There is a story about him that reveals the kind of man he really was.

The teenage daughter of a friend of his died suddenly one night. Early the next morning the man heard a knock on his door, and, when he opened it, there was Mr. Rayburn standing outside. The Speaker said, "I just came by to see what I could do to help."

The father replied in his deep grief, "I don't think there is anything you can do, Mr. Speaker. We are making all the arrangements."

"Well," Mr. Rayburn said, "have you had your coffee this morning?"

The man replied that they had not taken time for breakfast. So Mr. Rayburn said that he could at least make coffee for them. While he was working in the kitchen, the man came in and said, "Mr. Speaker, I thought you were supposed to be having breakfast at the White House this morning."

"Well, I was," Mr. Rayburn said, "but I called the President and told him I had a friend who was in trouble, and I couldn't come."[8]

These types of friends respond to our trouble in the same way God responds to ours. As Paul said in 2 Corinthians 1:4, we're to comfort others with the same kind of comfort we ourselves have received.

How many ways we can comfort someone! Sometimes just our presence does so much or a hand on the shoulder or a listening ear or a cup of coffee.

A Praying Friend

The apostle Paul reserved his richest comments for the man without whom the church of Colossae and the epistle of Colossians would not have existed—Epaphras. I've mentioned him throughout our study, because according to Colossians 1:7, this was the man who first took the Gospel to Colossae and whose concern about false teachers caused him to plead with Paul to write to the Colossians.

In Colossians 4:12-13, this man comes up again, and included in these verses are some of the New Testament's richest teachings about prayer: "Epaphras, who is one of you, a bondservant of Christ, greets you, always laboring fervently for you in prayers, that you may stand perfect and complete in all the will of God. For I bear him witness that he has a great zeal for you, and those who are in Laodicea, and those in Hierapolis."

Epaphras was a "bondservant of Christ," and he was passionate about two things: prayer and the people he prayed for! As he visited Paul in Rome, the great apostle was moved by watching and listening as Epaphras prayed fervently and with great zeal. Let's unpack four adverbs from Epaphras' life of prayer and apply them to ourselves.

He Prayed Faithfully

First, Epaphras prayed faithfully. Notice the word "always" in verse 12. While he was away from his friends in Colossae, Epaphras was constantly praying for them. The most interesting thing to me about the directives in the New Testament on prayer is not that we are told to pray, but to continue in prayer. We're to pray without ceasing. It can be hard enough just to begin praying, but Paul wants us to continue in it.

The moment we bring a request to the Lord, He never forgets it. But He loves for us to pray faithfully over the things He brings to our hearts. It's not because we're afraid He hasn't heard our past pleas. It's like talking to your best Friend.

There are certain issues or concerns that, when discussed in a healthy way, improve the friendship and the support that comes from it.

He Prayed Fiercely

The word "laboring" is sometimes translated as "wrestling." The New International Version says, "Epaphras, who is one of you and a servant of Christ Jesus, sends greetings. He is always wrestling in prayer for you" (verse 12).

The sport of wrestling has been around for a long time, and some people say it's the most exhausting sport of all because it requires you to use all the muscles in your body for an extended period of time. Often the winner of the match is the wrestler with the greatest energy level and stamina.

One wrestling coach said about a six-minute wrestling round, "There is nothing tougher to do in high school. And I challenge anyone to think something is tougher .... I don't care if it's football, lacrosse, swimming. There is nothing tougher. I've had more than a dozen kids that have gone off to Marine boot camp come back and say wrestling was tougher. And that's coming from guys that are adults now."[9]

Do you remember the story of Jacob wrestling with the angel of the Lord in Genesis 32? Jacob wrestled with God all night and refused to let go until he received his blessing. That was a fierce struggle, one that required persistence and endurance.

Prayer is hard work. It requires labor, striving, continuance, endurance, wrestling, and faithfulness. I've heard people say, "I would pray more but it's so hard." At least they understood the nature of prayer. Sometimes it helps to begin our prayers by confessing we don't feel like praying and asking God to help us with our preferences to be doing something else. Be honest with God and ask Him to give you a willingness to do the work of prayer.

He Prayed Fervently

The New King James Version adds the word "fervently." It says Epaphras was "always laboring fervently for you" (verse 12).

The word "fervent" means "to stretch, train or reach out." There's a difference between a typical Christian and a fervent Christian. Sometimes a fervent Christian's excitement exceeds their knowledge, especially in the case of new believers. You speak with them and discover that they don't know a lot, but they are very excited about what they do know. I would rather be around someone who is excited about the little they know than someone who is passive and cynical about how much they know.

Fervency is part of the ethos of the New Testament. Apollos was a preacher of whom it was said that he was "fervent in Spirit" (Acts 18:25). When Peter was in prison, the church was in "constant prayer" for him (Acts 12:5). And James 5:16 says, "The effective, fervent prayer of a righteous man avails much."

Some of us remember the week-long "revivals" that occurred once or twice a year in churches. Sometimes the buildings were packed every night, and many people came to Christ. Few churches have these protracted meetings now, but don't tell that to Pastor James Pritchard of Lafayette, Louisiana.

He scheduled a four-night revival, but the most important part of the meeting happened long before the opening night.

Pritchard told his church that the Holy Spirit moves in answer to fervent prayer. During a forty-day period, three hundred church members engaged in times of prayer and fasting, and Pritchard led the church in focused times of prayer during the Sunday services leading up to the meetings. On the Wednesday night before the revival, "cottage prayer meetings" took place at the church.

"We can do all the planning we want to do," said Pritchard, "and it can come to nothing. So, we knew for us to have any type of success we had to be praying …. We put up the sails, but it was up to Him to make the wind blow."

What happened? Every night saw more and more people coming to Christ. Sunday brought a record attendance of 888 people, and 56 people were baptized, ranging in age from 6 to 95 years old.[10]

Let's do all we can to erect the sails, but let's pray fervently for God to send the winds of the Holy Spirit to revive and bless our lives and our labor for Him!

He Prayed Factually

Finally, Epaphras prayed factually. The New Living Translation says, "Epaphras …. Always prays earnestly for you, asking God to make you strong and perfect, fully confident that you are following the whole will of God" (verse 12).

As we've seen, Gnostic heretics were infiltrating the church at Colossae with all their sophisticated philosophies and ideologies. They wanted to knock the theological feet out

from under the saints. Epaphras knew the only way
would survive this doctrinal attack was if they
perfect and complete in the will of God. Truth protec.
Church from the schemes of the devil.

I can't imagine a better prayer to offer for someone. Let me
challenge you to select a child, grandchild, or friend and put
their name in this verse. Begin praying it regularly for them:
"Lord, I pray earnestly for _____. I'm asking You to make
them strong and mature and confident. May they follow the
whole will of God in every decision and through every day."

A Talented Friend

Do you recall earlier I said Paul included Mark, the writer
of the second Gospel, in his list of friends? Well, the writer
of the third Gospel also shows up here. Colossians 4:14 says,
"Luke the beloved physician and Demas greet you."

Luke was a respected and important man in the Early
Church. He was probably a Gentile, yet wrote not only the
Gospel of Luke but also the book of Acts. If we go simply by
word count, Luke wrote more of the New Testament than
anyone else.

Luke was a physician and beloved by Paul. Medicine was
important to the Greeks, and physicians were held in high
esteem in that culture—much like ours. So here was Paul's
personal physician and coworker in ministry.

Luke first joined Paul at Troas in Acts 16:10. The good
doctor traveled with Paul to Jerusalem (Acts 20:5) and was
with him on the voyage to Rome (Acts 27:1). As a Christian
doctor, Luke would have been able to provide Paul not just

personal encouragement for the soul, but also healing advice for the body. What a blessing for Paul!

At the end of Paul's life, we get the most moving portrait of what Luke meant to Paul. In Paul's final book, he wrote from Rome's death row, "Only Luke is with me" (2 Timothy 4:11).

Luke the physician was a talented and respected man. He was an author, historian, and physician. And he used all of those skills to serve the Lord. But most of all he was a faithful friend to Paul, a friend who stayed with him until the end.

Proverbs 18:24 says, "There is a friend who sticks closer than a brother."

Again, the question isn't whether we have such a friend; it's whether we are such a friend. Dr. Amir Levine, a psychiatrist and a neuroscientist and the author of *Attached: The New Science of Adult Attachment and How It Can Help You Find and Keep Love*, wrote, "Social connections are the most powerful way for us to regulate our emotional distress. If you are in distress, being in proximity to someone you're securely attached to is the most effective way to calm yourself."[11]

A Difficult Friend

There's one discouraging spot in Paul's friendship list in Colossians, but we only learn about it by studying his other books. It's Demas. Look at Colossians 4:14 again: "Luke the beloved physician and Demas greet you."

Demas is mentioned three times in Paul's letters, and the progression tells a difficult story. In Philemon 23-24, Paul called him a fellow laborer and included him in a list of four other good men. Here in Colossians, Paul simply mentioned his name without any special word of praise or appreciation.

The final reference describes what eventually happened to the relationship between the two. In Paul's final known letter he wrote, "Demas has forsaken me, having loved this present world, and has departed for Thessalonica" (2 Timothy 4:10).

Sometimes friends walk away from us. They may also walk away from Christ. This is one of life's most difficult experiences. If this has happened to you, please remember it happened to the apostle Paul as well, and at the very end of his life and ministry. It also happened to Jesus.

Without a doubt, the most painful use of the word "friend" in the Bible took place in Matthew 26:50, when our Lord's disciple, Judas, led the enemy forces right to Jesus, who was praying in the Garden of Gethsemane. As the torches illuminated the chilly night and the clanging of soldiers woke the disciples, Jesus looked up and saw Judas, who was ready to identify and betray the Savior with a kiss.

"Friend," Jesus said to him, "why have you come?"

If the apostle Paul and even Jesus Himself could survive a friend's betrayal or abandonment, so can you if you'll remember that we have a Friend who will never leave us or forsake us.

A Hospitable Friend

Turning from Demas, we next encounter a happier friend, a hospitable one. Colossians 4:15-16 says, "Greet the brethren who are in Laodicea, and Nymphas and the church that is in his house. Now when this epistle is read among you, see that it is read also in the church of the Laodiceans, and that you likewise read the epistle from Laodicea."

Some ancient versions say, "her house," so we're not sure if Nymphas was a man or a woman. Nymphas must have been a mature and hospitable leader in the church, someone who enjoyed entertaining people and bringing friends together. The type of friend who multiplies the friendships in your life.

Let me tell you about someone who experienced this gift in blessed reverse.

Judith Heicksen of Santa, Idaho, went through a season in life that exhausted her every nerve. She and her husband had moved two thousand miles from their family with their toddler. When Judith had another baby, there were complications. The child had severely clubbed feet. Suddenly Judith was taking care of two small children, one requiring constant medical attention with endless doctor's appointments. Judith struggled with fatigue and fell behind on all her housework.

"One day," she wrote, "we came home from yet another doctor's visit to find the front door ajar. I cautiously proceeded into the house, only to find the floors spotless, the dishes cleaned and dried, and the dirty laundry washed and folded. Upstairs, the beds were made, and there were even flowers in a vase beside my bed.

"It turns out that my friend Joy was driving by my home and noticed my car was gone, so she took the opportunity to help me out," Judith said. "I learned an important lesson that day about compassion. And this friendship was sealed for life!"[12]

I want to say one final word about Colossians 4:16. Paul mentions a letter he wrote to the Laodiceans. This letter has been lost to us. If you're like me, you'd love to know what Paul said in this lost letter. But remember, Paul was a constant letter writer. He undoubtedly wrote hundreds or thousands of letters during his lifetime. The Holy Spirit inspired and preserved thirteen for us. The Lord knew we'd be overwhelmed with too much, and so He breathed His own word through thirteen pieces of Paul's correspondence—and that's why we so treasure the Pauline epistles, from Romans to Philemon.

A Discouraged Friend

Finally, let's touch on Paul's tenth friend—a discouraged man. Colossians 4:17-18 says, "And say to Archippus, 'Take heed to the ministry which you have received in the Lord, that you may fulfill it.' This salutation by my own hand—Paul. Remember my chains. Grace be with you. Amen."

The New International Version says: "Tell Archippus: 'See to it that you complete the ministry you have received in the Lord.'"

Warren Wiersbe wrote, "When we compare Colossians 4:17 with Philemon 2, we get the impression that Archippus belonged to the family of Philemon. Possibly, he was Philemon's son and the pastor of the church that met in Philemon's house .... Paul's last words before his salutation are directed at Archippus as an encouragement to continue faithfully in his ministry. Was Archippus discouraged? Had the gnostic false teachers invaded his church and created problems for him? We do not know. But we do know that pastors of local churches face many problems and carry many burdens, and they often need a word of encouragement."

Wiersbe continued, "Paul reminded Archippus that his ministry was a gift from God, and that he was a steward of God who would one day have to give an account of his work. Since the Lord gave him his ministry, the Lord could also help him carry it out in the right way."[13]

Do you ever need a reminder to complete the task God has assigned you?

Dr. John Dunlop, a medical doctor, geriatrist, and professor, wrote a book entitled *Finishing Well to the Glory of God*. He often had patients who came to his office for a physical exam prior to their retirement. Dr. Dunlop always shared two rules for maintaining an active and meaningful life: (1) "Wake up every morning knowing what you are going to do that day;" and (2) "Go to bed every night knowing that you helped someone."[14]

Think of every single day as a fresh period of time when we can be about our Father's business. Ask Him what He wants you to do, and do your work in one-day increments. If we earnestly seek to walk daily and work daily with the Lord, we'll finish the work He has assigned us and He will tell us, "Well done!"

Share that vision with a discouraged friend, and see if you can help spur them on to good works!

And with that we come to the last verse of Colossians: "I, Paul, write this greeting in my own hand. Remember my chains. Grace be with you" (4:18, NIV).

It's almost certain Paul dictated this book to someone who transcribed it, but at the end he himself took the quill and wrote the final words. He poignantly said, "Remember my chains."

The nineteenth-century Dean of Canterbury, Henry Alford, wrote [his signature]: "When we read of his chains we should not forget that they moved over the paper as he wrote. His hand was chained to the soldier that kept him .... It is as if he said: 'This is not a letter from someone who does not know what the service of Christ means or someone who is asking others to do what he is not prepared to do himself. It is a letter from one who has himself suffered and sacrificed for Christ. My only right to speak is that I too have carried the cross of Christ.'"[15]

"Grace be with you," Paul wrote. "Amen."

As we close our study of the book of Colossians, my heart is filled with gratitude for Paul and his ten Gospel friends. We owe them so much! I'm thankful for their lives and ministries. Without them we wouldn't have been able to experience the supremacy and sufficiency of Jesus Christ.

He gives us all we need—the work we need, the hope we need, the strength we need, the forgiveness we need, and the heaven we need. Above us and beyond us and before us is the Son who is the Image of God, the Firstborn over all creation. For in Him all things were created on earth and in heaven, visible and invisible, and He is our glorious and preeminent Lord who makes known to us His glorious riches.

Christ in you, the hope of glory!

Readers' Guide

For Personal Reflection

Settle into your favorite chair with your Bible, a pen or pencil, and this book. Read a chapter, marking portions that seem significant to you. Write in the margins. Note where you agree, disagree, or question the author. Look up endnotes and relevant Scripture passages. Then turn to the questions listed in this study guide. If you want to trace your progress with a written record, use a notebook to record your answers, thoughts, feelings, and further questions. Refer to the text and to the Scriptures as you allow the questions to enlarge your thinking. And most importantly, pray. Ask God to give you a discerning mind for truth, an active concern for others, and a greater love for Him.

For Group Study

Plan ahead. Before meeting with your group, read and mark the chapter as if you were preparing for personal study. Glance through the questions, making mental notes of how you might contribute to your group's discussion. Bring a Bible and the text to your meeting.

Arrange an environment that promotes discussion. Comfortable chairs arranged in a casual circle invite people to talk with each other. They say, "We are here to listen and respond to each other—and to learn together." If you are the leader, simply be sure to sit where you can have eye contact with each person.

Promptness counts. Time is as valuable to many people as money. If the group runs late (because of a late start), these people will feel as robbed as if you had picked their pockets. So, unless you have mutual agreement, begin and end on time.

Involve everyone. Group learning works best if everyone participates more or less equally. If you are a natural talker, pause before you enter the conversation. Then ask a quiet person what he or she thinks. If you are a natural listener, don't hesitate to jump into the discussion. Others will benefit from your thoughts—but only if you speak them. If you are the leader, be careful not to dominate the session. Of course, you will have thought about the study ahead of time, but don't assume that people are present just to hear you—as flattering as that may feel. Instead, help group members to make their own discoveries. Ask the questions, but insert your own ideas only as they are needed to fill gaps.

Pace the study. The questions for each session are designed to last about one hour. Early questions form the framework for later discussion, so don't rush by so quickly that you miss valuable foundation material. Later questions, however, often speak of the here and now. So don't dawdle so long at the beginning that you leave no time to "get personal." While the leader must take responsibility for timing the flow of questions, it is the job of each person in the group to assist in keeping the study moving at an even pace.

Pray for each other—together or alone. Then watch God's hand at work in all of your lives. Notice that each session includes the following features:

Session Topic—a brief statement summarizing the session.

Community Builder—an activity to get acquainted with the session topic and/or with each other.

Discovery Questions—a list of questions to encourage individual or group discovery and application.

Prayer Focus—suggestions for turning one's learning into prayer.

Optional Activities—supplemental ideas that will enhance the study.

Assignment—activities or preparation to complete prior to the next session.

CHAPTER 1 - SINGING THE PRAISES OF THE UNSUNG
COLOSSIANS 1:1-8

Session Topic

Faithful living—it's all about Christ.

Community Builder (Choose One)

1. Who is someone you know whose faith has been a great example for you? What about their life and the way they have lived out their faith has made an impact on you?

2. What is it about faithful service that deflects away from us and toward Christ? How can we live more like that?

Discovery Questions

1. Read aloud Colossians 1:1-8. How does Paul describe the Colossian church and the ministry taking place there?

2. How many times does this passage reference God and Christ? How does this help emphasize the centrality of God in Paul's letter and in the Colossian church?

3. What does Paul call the Colossians? (verse 2) What does that mean for us?

4. What does the faith of the Colossians look like?

5. How can we live with that kind of faith? How would that be different from how we are living now?

6. Paul commends the Colossians' "love for all the saints" in verse 4. How can we be more faithful to love all of the Christians in our lives and treat them like the Colossians treated their fellow believers?

7. Where does verse 5 say our hope is "laid up"? How should that change our daily outlook on life?

8. What does Paul remind the Colossians of in verse 6? How can we use that to refocus our lives and live out our mission for God?

9. Look forward to the next few sections of Colossians 1. How do verses 5 and 6 prepare us to read those sections?

10. What do we learn about Epaphras in verse 7? Would someone describe us that way? If not, what can we do to change that?

Prayer Focus

- Paul describes the Colossians' faith in great detail: They love Christ and their fellow Christians, their hope is in heaven with their minds set on the Gospel, and the Gospel is producing fruit in their lives and ministry. Ask God to renew your focus on Him and to guide you in His will so you may also produce fruit according to the Gospel.

- Paul says in verse 3 that he and his companions are "praying always" for the Colossian church. Take a moment to think of a missionary, ministry, church, or people group and pray for them. If you are willing, commit to praying for them multiple times a day this week.

- Pray that God will help you to be an Epaphras this week: a dear servant and faithful minister of Christ.

Optional Activities

1. After reading about Paul, Timothy, and Epaphras, think about faithful believers in your life who share some of the qualities of these people discussed in this chapter. Take time to think about how you can take one aspect of these people's lives and try to live it out this week.

2. Think back to how we defined a saint in this chapter (any sinner saved by grace). If you are a saint, think about how this changes the way you are called to live

your life. What attitudes, actions, and words should be brought before God for His grace and forgiveness?

Assignment

1. Keep a journal of everything you learn from the book of Colossians, starting with verses 1-8 that we studied today. Each week write down in your Colossians journal what stands out to you in the passage, and pray that God would help you to take in those truths and live them out as well.

2. Memorize Colossians 1:5-6. Meditate on this passage throughout the week, and look for opportunities to share the Gospel and bear its fruit.

Chapter 2 - Wisdom and Understanding
Colossians 1:9-14

Session Topic
Praying for wisdom—so we might walk worthy of the Lord.

Community Builder (Choose One)
1. Think about a time in which you needed wisdom that you didn't have. How would biblical wisdom have made a difference in the situation?

2. Name a popular person who always acts and speaks with wisdom. Now think of one who seemingly never acts and speaks with wisdom. How many differences can you think of between the two?

Discovery Questions
1. Read aloud Colossians 1:9-14. How many verses does the first sentence of Paul's prayer stretch across? What can we learn from this about the depth of Paul's prayer?

2. What does Paul say about his prayers for the Colossians in verse 9? Do we ever pray without ceasing like this?

3. How does Paul describe God's will in verse 9? How do we live differently when we are actively seeking God's will for our lives?

4. When Paul prays for the Colossians to "walk worthy of the Lord" in verse 10, what do you think that means?

5. What are some common ways that we often fail to do this? How can we challenge each other to do better?

6. How are being fruitful and increasing in knowledge connected? Can we be more fruitful without learning more about God?

7. Knowing all of the suffering that Paul faced throughout his ministry, how important do you think it was

for him to write about being joyful in patience and longsuffering? (verse 11) Why is it so hard for us to have joy in suffering?

8. Read verse 12 again. What does it say God has qualified us to be? What is the "inheritance of the saints" Paul references?

9. Verse 13 talks about the conveying (transferring) of us from darkness into His Kingdom. How significant is this for the rest of the passage? Which parts of this passage would we be able to accomplish without this work of God?

10. Paul reminds the Colossians of the redemption they have in Christ. Why is it so important to keep returning to this truth? What does that mean for us today?

Prayer Focus

- God has provided us redemption through His Son, and now He offers us wisdom and understanding in Him! Spend some time thinking about the seriousness of this sacrifice and all of its implications, and then thank God for His wonderful sacrifice and continual redemption of our minds and hearts through the wisdom He offers us.

- Take a moment to reflect on how your walk with Christ has been recently. Ask God for forgiveness in areas you have failed, and then ask God to help you walk worthy of Him.

- Pray for joy in moments of suffering. Ask for help in being aware of the joy of the Lord, despite your temporary circumstances and how you feel.

Optional Activities

1. Think about one area in your life that you need more wisdom in. Make a game plan to pray for wisdom each day and ask a friend to join you in praying.

2. Ask someone if you can teach them what you have learned about Colossians 1:9-14. Pray that God will use it to teach and encourage you and the person you teach.

Assignment

1. Break the passage up into seven sections, and commit to praying through each portion of the passage multiple times throughout each day.

2. Memorize Colossians 1:13-14.

3. Continue writing in your Colossians journal as you record what God's Word says and how He speaks to you through it.

CHAPTER 3 - THE FULLNESS OF CHRIST
COLOSSIANS 1:15-23

Session Topic
The Person of Christ—who He is and what He has done.

Community Builder (Choose One)
1. What is your favorite sermon you have heard about Christ? What specifically stuck out about His nature or works that made you remember it even today?

2. Name the person you can think of who has the most degrees, accomplishments, and awards attached to their name. How does that compare with the long list of truths about Christ's Person and works?

Discovery Questions
1. Read aloud Colossians 1:15-23. What does verse 15 say about Christ's relationship with creation? How does this help us understand Him better?

2. How was Christ involved in the creation process? (verse 16)

3. When verse 16 says all things were created "for [Christ]," how should that change the way we live?

4. Verse 17 says in Jesus "all things consist." What does this say about Jesus' power over the world?

5. How can we use the body metaphor for the Church with Christ as the Head to better live as individual parts of the Body of Christ?

6. What do verses 19 and 20 say about being reconciled to God? What is the condition for this reconciliation? (verse 20)

7. Paul talks in verse 21 about the previous wicked state of the Colossians' minds. How does the work of Jesus change our minds and renew us?

8. What three things does Christ's death in His earthly body accomplish? (verse 22)

9. Paul tells us in verse 23 to continue to be "grounded and steadfast" in our faith. What are a few ways we can focus on growing our faith more this week so our faith will look like that?

10. Paul warns the Colossians to continue on in the hope of the Gospel and not be moved away by it. How can we stay anchored in this hope?

Prayer Focus

- Paul talks about the transformation of the Colossians in verse 21 from alienation to reconciliation. Take some time in thankful prayer to meditate on this truth and thank God for sending His Son so we might enter a into right relationship with Him.

- Ask God to help you always be meditating on this passage about Jesus and the work He has done, is doing, and will do. Pray for acknowledgement of this work as it is happening, that you might see God working actively in your life.

Optional Activities

1. Re-read verse 22. This week, journal times in which God helps you to be "holy, and blameless, and above reproach" as you seek to live for Him. Praise God for these moments and thank Him for His willingness to work through you.

2. Reflect on the two categories of "Who He Is" and "What He Does." Make a list of all the facts about Jesus

discussed in this chapter and organize them into these two categories. Hang it up where you can look at it all day and continue to be reminded of those truths.

Assignment

1. Seek out three people this week whom you can share the Gospel with, telling them about who Jesus is and what He has done, both for all humanity and for you personally.

2. Create a chapter 3 entry for your Colossians journal and write down the verses about the Person and works of Christ that seemed most important to the passage and to you personally.

Chapter 4 - True or False?
Colossians 1:24–2:7

Session Topic
The commitments and concerns of Christian ministry—what is the cost?

Community Builder (Choose One)
1. Name someone who embodies sacrificial service in his or her life. What makes this person so special?

2. Think about a person who has helped you grow in Christ. What about their witness and encouragement helped you grow?

Discovery Questions
1. Read aloud Colossians 1:24–2:7. Paul says in verse 24 that he fills up in his "flesh what is lacking in the afflictions of Christ." What does this mean with regards to taking up our crosses and suffering for Christ?

2. What is the mystery Paul talks about in verse 26? (Look ahead to verse 27.)

3. How does this revelation give us urgency in our witness?

4. Paul preaches "Christ in you, the hope of glory." (verse 27) What do we need to do in order to better live with this hope as the motivation for our daily life?

5. What simple preaching and evangelistic model does Paul give in verse 28?

6. Verse 29 says we work for Christ, as He also works in us. How important is it in light of this verse to stay close to God and His Word?

7. What does Paul warn against in Colossians 2:4? How can we be on guard against this?

8. Verse 6 commands us to "walk in Him." What does this look like practically?

9. Paul's final thought in this passage is to do all he has said with thanksgiving. What effect does living thankfully and always having a thankful attitude have on our lives and ministry?

Prayer Focus

- Paul teaches the Colossians to share the mystery of Christ which has now been revealed. Pray that God would soften people's hearts to be receptive to the Gospel and that He would give you opportunities to share it.

- Pray this week that God will keep you from being deceived with persuasive words (as Colossians 2:4 warns against). Ask God to keep you close to His Word and His truth.

Optional Activities

1. Put your name in verse 29, right after "I." For example: "To this end I, _____, also labor, striving according to His working which works in me mightily." Write this down and place it on your mirror or somewhere prominent.

2. Paul begins with a note on rejoicing in suffering and ends with a call to do what he has said with thanksgiving. Take a moment before each difficult situation you enter into this week to pray about rejoicing in suffering and living a thankful life to God's glory.

Assignment

1. Continue your Colossians journal and write down how God has spoken to you this week through this passage.

2. Memorize Colossians 2:6-7.

CHAPTER 5 - BEWARE
COLOSSIANS 2:8-23

Session Topic
Staying close to the truth of Christ, not the lies of the world.

Community Builder (Choose One)
1. Tell the group about a time when someone tried to cheat you out of something through empty words and lies.

2. List some examples of Christians throughout history who have gone wrong in their teaching. Think about what might have caused that, and brainstorm how we can stay away from those temptations.

Discovery Questions
1. Read aloud Colossians 2:8-23. Paul begins with a warning in verse 8. What is his warning, and what might that look like in our lives?

2. Verses 9-10 say we are "complete" in Christ. How does this change our attitudes toward the world?

3. How do we put off the body of flesh that Paul talks about in verse 11?

4. Verses 13 and 14 deal with the forgiveness of Christ to wipe away all our sins. What does this mean for us as we seek to live by His grace and not by our works?

5. What does verse 16 say about the judgment of others? How can we better seek God's approval over the approval of others?

6. What warning does Paul give in verse 18? How can we steer away from that temptation?

7. How does Paul say we can grow in faith in verse 19? What connection is that growth dependent upon?

8. Paul urges the Colossians not to live by the rituals of the world in verses 20-22. What rituals might we be tempted to follow today, and how can we stand by Paul's words and fight against them?

9. Paul ends by noting the worldly value of things having an "appearance of wisdom." How can we be careful not to live by the rituals of this world, but rather to stay anchored in the truth of Christ?

Prayer Focus
- Paul warns against five temptations that lead away from God and toward man-made systems. Ask God to help you steer away from these false teachings and to stay connected to Christ, the Head of the Body.

- Pray for God to give you strength to rely on Him alone and not on the ways of this world.

Optional Activities
1. Write down the five aspects of the Gnostic heresy Paul countered in this passage: intellectualism, ritualism, legalism, mysticism, and asceticism. Study these issues and write down modern examples of these that confuse Christians and distract them from Christ.

2. Choose one verse from this passage that particularly stuck out to you, and share it with someone who it might encourage or help.

Assignment
1. Write down chapter 5 in your Colossians journal. Take this moment to reflect on the first half of the book, what it has taught you, and how you have been able to implement that in your life.

2. Memorize Colossians 2:9-10.

CHAPTER 6 - WHAT IT MEANS TO BE "IN CHRIST"
COLOSSIANS 3:1-11

Session Topic
Our new life as a follower of Christ must be filled with godly qualities.

Community Builder (Choose One)
1. Think about a time when your mind was focused on the wrong things. What was the result?

2. List some things that can distract us from Christ.

Discovery Questions
1. Read aloud Colossians 3:1-11. What does it mean to "seek those things which are above" in verse 1? How can we do that?

2. Why is it so important to set our minds on things above and not on the earth?

3. How does verse 4 say we will appear when Christ returns?

4. Verse 5 gives a list of sinful desires. What can we do this week to avoid these?

5. Verse 6 says God's wrath will come on those who live in these sins. How does this show God's standard of justice?

6. How are we different in Christ than before we were in Christ? (verse 7)

7. What do you think the Church would look like if we all put off the list of sins Paul gives in verse 8?

8. How do we often fail to live up to that standard, and what are the consequences?

9. Verses 9-10 say we have taken off the old man and put on the new man. What does that mean?

10. Paul ends by saying "Christ is all and in all." How does this relate to the beginning of verse 11?

Prayer Focus

- Ask God to help you grow closer to Him and further away from the sins that can distract us from God.

- Pray for God to help you live as the new man this week, taking off the old man and his sins.

Optional Activities

1. Paul gives five sins to avoid in verse 8. Choose one of these you struggle with, and intentionally pray about this sin and ask someone close to you to keep you accountable in this area.

2. Find a way this week to share with someone that Christ is all and in all, greater than any barriers of this world.

Assignment

1. Fill out chapter 6 in your Colossians journal and continue to record those things most important to your understanding of the book of Colossians

2. Memorize Colossians 3:2.

CHAPTER 7 - THE CHRISTIAN'S DRESS CODE
COLOSSIANS 3:12-17

Session Topic

We must live with a Christlike character since we have been saved by Him and for Him.

Community Builder (Choose One)

1. When is a time that you have seen someone dramatically change their life? What was the result?

2. What are some things you used to do before you accepted Christ? How is the new you different?

Discovery Questions

1. Read aloud Colossians 3:12-17. What does Paul tell the Colossians to put on in verse 12?

2. How does this differ from the tendencies of the world around us?

3. How does Paul tell the Colossians to interact with one another in verse 13?

4. In what ways are we guilty of not living like this? How have we done this well?

5. What does Paul say love is the bond of in verse 14?

6. How does this represent the love of God working in this world to redeem it?

7. Paul emphasizes living with peace and thankfulness. Why is it so easy to be argumentative and ungrateful?

8. In verse 16, Paul instructs the believers on the "word of Christ." How can our churches better focus on the Word?

9. What does it look like when we are all singing and teaching one another in the Word?

10. How can we take verse 17 seriously and "do all in the name of the Lord Jesus"?

Prayer Focus

- Ask God to help you put on the attributes of Christ listed in this passage.

- Call on God's peace to rule in your heart and drive your words and actions. Ask for guidance in living for Him.

Optional Activities

1. Ask a trusted Christian friend to share some biblical wisdom with you about a way in which you can be more Christlike.

2. Look up practical ways Christians have sought to live as a new person in Christ. Take one of these and commit to trying it for a week.

Assignment

1. Write out chapter 7 in your Colossians journal and spend time in prayer over the lessons God is teaching you. Make sure these words you are hearing are also being lived out.

2. Memorize Colossians 3:16.

CHAPTER 8 - THE CHRISTIAN HOUSEHOLD
COLOSSIANS 3:18–4:1

Session Topic
The family of God must live with respect to one another with Christ at the center.

Community Builder (Choose One)
1. What has been your experience with family and work interactions? How can they go wrong?

2. Name someone who does an exceptional job at loving their spouse, obeying their parents, or working well at their job. What qualities make them like this?

Discovery Questions
1. Read aloud Colossians 3:18–4:1. What are some common misconceptions about this passage in today's culture?

2. How can we seek to be faithful to the Bible and also answer people's concerns about this passage?

3. What instruction does Paul give to wives? How is this different from some people's view of submission?

4. What instruction does Paul give to husbands? How do husbands often fail to live like this?

5. Paul says it is "pleasing to the Lord" for children to obey their parents. Why is this so different from the attitude of many children?

6. Is Paul approving of the relationship between servant and master, or is he simply giving instructions on how people of every status should serve God in their relationships?

7. How does Paul tell servants and masters to treat one another? How does this compare to the attitudes of many employees and employers?

8. What is one practical way we can be a witness at work this week by acting as Paul tells employees to act?

9. Whom does Paul say we are ultimately serving? (verse 23) How does this change our actions and attitudes?

10. What is the inheritance Paul speaks of in verse 24? How can this motivate us to live for God in our relationships?

Prayer Focus

- Ask God to give you strength and wisdom in your relationships this week, so that whomever you interact with, you are serving them as you also serve the Lord.

- Pray for the willingness to submit to this teaching and the ability to live according to God's Word. Ask for His grace in areas you continue to struggle in with regards to this.

Optional Activities

1. Have a conversation with someone close to you whom you don't always treat well. Ask for forgiveness for those times, and share with them the lesson you have learned from this passage and how you want to live that out.

2. Write down three relationships you have that could use this passage's teaching. Try to live as Paul has commanded us to in this passage, and journal the difference it makes as you act this way.

Assignment

1. Fill out chapter 8 in your Colossians journal. Make special note of the relationship dynamics mentioned, how they differ from the world's advice, and how they show the love of Christ.

2. Memorize Colossians 3:23-24.

Chapter 9 - Christian Communication
Colossians 4:2-6

Session Topic
How do we interact with those who are "outside"?

Community Builder (Choose One)
1. Who is someone who speaks gracefully and truthfully in your life? What can you learn from them?

2. Name a time when God worked powerfully through your prayers or the prayers of someone you know. What effect did this have on you?

Discovery Questions
1. Read aloud Colossians 4:2-6. What do we know about how the Bible calls us to interact with those who are not Christians? How can we use that to help us as we begin to study this passage on the same topic?

2. Paul calls us in verse 2 to "continue earnestly in prayer." How can this simple command lead to bold faith?

3. Whom do you know that is vigilant in their earnest prayer, and how can we learn from that?

4. What does Paul mean when he says to pray with thanksgiving? In what ways can we be more thankful in prayer?

5. Paul asks the Colossians to pray for him. What specific opportunity does he ask them to pray for?

6. How can we be diligent in staying connected to people who would have this same prayer request?

7. What does Paul mean in verse 4 when he says, "that I may make it manifest"?

8. Paul ends verse 4 with the statement "as I ought to speak." What does this say about our call to preach the Gospel?

9. Paul speaks with urgency about using his time well. How can wisdom lead us to make the most of the time we have with those who do not know Christ?

10. How can we balance proclaiming the truth of Christ with the grace Paul tells us to speak with? Are grace and truth in contrast to one another?

Prayer Focus

- Ask God to help you be fully focused on living your Christian life well, taking every opportunity to pray for those who need Christ and sharing your faith with them whenever you can.

- Pray for grace as you speak with those who do not know the Lord, answering their questions with the truth in love.

Optional Activities

1. Meditate on Colossians 4:5-6. Think about a few people you know who need to receive Christ, and try to think of ways you can share Christ with them this week.

2. Read a little bit about a famous missionary today. What did their speech sound like, and how were they able to effectively share the Gospel?

Assignment

1. Continue writing in your Colossians journal. As we begin to conclude the book of Colossians, take a moment to pray fervently that God will help you to retain all you have learned and that you would implement it in your life.

2. Memorize Colossians 4:6.

CHAPTER 10 - PAUL AND HIS FRIENDS
COLOSSIANS 4:7-18

Session Topic
Godly friends encourage one another in the faith and increase their work in ministry.

Community Builder (Choose One)
1. Name a time that a friend meant a lot to you. Are you being a friend like this to others?

2. What is the role of friendships in the Bible? Who are some prominent friends that stick out to you in the Bible?

Discovery Questions
1. Read aloud Colossians 4:7-18. How does Paul describe Tychicus?

2. How can we better live as friends like Tychicus was to Paul?

3. Read Philemon 8-16. How does Paul describe Onesimus?

4. How can we live more like Onesimus, a friend of Paul's who received great praise?

5. After Paul lists numerous people in verses 10-11, he talks about the comfort they have provided him. What is the importance of having godly friends to support you, especially in a situation like Paul's?

6. How can we seek out godly friendship and create lasting relationships that strengthen us in our faith?

7. What does Epaphras pray on behalf of the Colossian believers? (verse 12)

8. How does Paul describe Epaphras in verse 13? How can we be more like that?

9. What message does Paul leave for Archippus in verse 17?

10. After reading in chapter 10 about the encouragement Paul gave Archippus through this message, what can we learn about the value of encouragement in ministry?

11. Whom can we encourage this week to remain steadfast in their ministry and confident in the Lord?

Prayer Focus

- Ask God to show you friends who need encouragement, and pray with those people.

- Pray for God to help you listen to the advice of godly friends and grow closer to Him through it.

- Paul says to remember his chains. Pray for the persecuted church today: over a particular missionary, ministry, or country who needs the Lord to work mightily in them.

Optional Activities

1. Make a list of three friends you can encourage this week. Spend time in prayer over them, and then reach out to them and ask how they are doing in their walk with the Lord.

2. Ask a friend for one piece of encouragement in your faith this week. Take that encouragement, and share it with someone else.

Assignment

1. Finalize your Colossians journal. Review each entry, and pray for God to continue speaking to you through His Word as He has done throughout this study.

2. Memorize Colossians 4:12.

Notes

INTRODUCTION: CHRIST ABOVE ALL

1. Chuck Toney, "Humble at the Top: Why These CEOs Still Write Thank You Notes," *Chick-fil-A*, March 10, 2017, https://www.chick-fil-a.com/storieslifestyle/humble-at-the-top-why-these-ceos-still-write-thank-you-notes.

2. A. T. Robertson, *The Student's Chronological New Testament* (New York, NY: Fleming H. Revell Company, 1904) xxxix.

CHAPTER 1: SINGING THE PRAISES OF THE UNSUNG

1. Kare Anderson, "Who Packs Your Parachute?" *Forbes*, November 18, 2015, https://www.forbes.com/sites/kareanderson/2015/11/18/who-packs-your-parachute/?sh=f76eec57a717d.

2. Merily Leis, "7 Stories That Prove The Importance of Teamwork," *Scoro*, https://www.scoro.com/blog/teamwork-stories-importance-of-teamwork/.

3. John Phillips, *Exploring Colossians & Philemon: An Expository Commentary* (Grand Rapids, MI: Kregel Publications, 2002), 16.

4. *Eusebius: The Church History*, translated by Paul L. Maier (Grand Rapids, MI: Kregel Publications, 1999), 93-94.

5. Quoted by J. Hampton Keathley III, "Mark #16: Accountability," *Bible.org*, https://bible.org/seriespage/mark-16-accountability.

6. Jon Gordon, *The Power of Positive Leadership* (Hoboken, NJ: John Wiley & Sons, Inc., 2017), Kindle Edition.

7. John Phillips, *Exploring Colossians & Philemon: An Expository Commentary* (Grand Rapids, MI: Kregel Publications, 2002), 18.

8. Adrian Rogers, "What Does It Mean To Be Faithful," *Love Worth Finding With Adrian Rogers*, https://www.lwf.org/fruit-of-the-spirit/what-does-it-mean-to-be-faithful.

9. John Phillips, *Exploring Colossians & Philemon: An Expository Commentary* (Grand Rapids, MI: Kregel Publications, 2002), 18-19.

10. Charles Spurgeon, "Strengthening Words from the Saviour's Lips," *The Spurgeon Center*, https://www.spurgeon.org/resource-library/sermons/strengthening-words-from-the-saviours-lips/#flipbook/.

11. R. Kent Hughes, *Colossians and Philemon: The Supremacy of Christ* (Wheaton, IL: Crossway Books, 1989), 15.

12. Walter B. Knight, *Knight's Master Book of New Illustrations* (Grand Rapids, MI: Eerdmans Publishing Company, 1956), 16.

13. Richard Sturz, *The Colportage Library: Studies in Colossians—The Preeminent Christ* (Chicago, IL: Moody Press, 1955), 22.

14. Mark Buchanan, *Hidden in Plain Sight: The Secret of More* (Nashville, TN: Thomas Nelson, 2007), Kindle Edition.

15. Warren Wiersbe, *Be Complete: Colossians* (Colorado Springs, CO: David C. Cook, 1981), 38.

16. Clark Cothern, "Our Inheritance, Kept in a Safe Place," *Preaching Today*, https://www.preachingtoday.com/search/?query=hope%20in%20heaven&contentFilter=Illustration.

17. David E. Garland, *Colossians/Philemon: The NIV Application Commentary* (Grand Rapids, MI: Zondervan Academic, 2009), 50.

18. Eduard Schweizer, *The Letter to the Colossians* (Minneapolis, MN: Augsburg Pub. House, 1982), 37.

19. Deann Alford, "New Life in a Culture of Death," *Christianity Today*, February 1, 2004, https://www.christianitytoday.com/ct/2004/february/5.48.html.

20. J. B. Lightfoot, *St. Paul's Epistles to the Colossians and Philemon* (Trinity College, Cambridge, 1875), Kindle Edition.

21. Renee Zou, "Moment-by-Moment Faithfulness," *The Gospel Coalition*, May 21, 2019, https://au.thegospelcoalition.org/article/moment-moment-faithfulness/.

CHAPTER 2: WISDOM AND UNDERSTANDING

1. Lois Neely, *Come Up to This Mountain* (Wheaton, IL: Tyndale, 1989), 65.

2. Patricia Sullivan, "'Christian Lady' Cleaned for 6 Presidents," *Washington Post*, June 21, 2009, https://www.washingtonpost.com.

3. A. T. Robertson, *Paul and the Intellectuals* (Nashville, TN: Broadman Press, 1956), 33.

4. Morgan Sloss, "People Are Sharing The Dumbest Things They've Seen Smart People Do, And I Can't Stop Laughing," *Buzzfeed*, July 16, 2021, https://www.buzzfeed.com/morgansloss1/dumb-fails-from-smart-people-reddit.

5. C. F. D. Moule, *The Epistles to the Colossians and to Philemon* (Cambridge: Cambridge University Press, 1957), 49.

6. Jay Blossom, "Mnemonic devices and the desires of our heart," *The Presbyterian Outlook*, June 5, 2021, https://pres-outlook.org/2021/07/mnemonic-devices-and-the-desires-of-our-hearts/.

7. Original source unknown.

8. Leonardo Blair, "Only 13% of Evangelicals Tithe, Half Give Away Less Than 1% of Income Annually: Study," *Christian Post*, October 29, 2021, https://www.christianpost.com/news/only-13-of-evangelicals-tithe-study.html.

9. Kent R. Hughes, *Preaching the Word: Colossians* (Wheaton, IL: Crossway Books, 1989), 25.

10. Steven Kovac, "Thankful cancer survivor 'chooses joy,'" *Sanila County News*, November 27, 2019, https://sanilaccountynews.mihomepaper.com/articles/thankful-cancer-survivor-chooses-joy/.

11. Ralph P. Martin, *Colossians and Philemon: The New Century Bible* (London: Oliphants, Marshall and Scott, 1978), 53.

12. W. H. Griffith Thomas, *Studies in Colossians and Philemon* (Grand Rapids, MI: Baker Book House, 1973), 36.

13. David E. Garland, *Colossians/Philemon: The NIV Application Commentary* (Grand Rapids, MI: Zondervan, 1998), Kindle Edition.

14. "A Life and Destiny Changed Forever Through a Scripture Found When Needed Most!" *The Gideon's International*, January 21, 2022, https://www.gideons.org/enews/n_2201_597_GEN_EN001/destiny_changed.

15. Sally Herships, "Lee Horton Reflects On Coming Home After Years In Prison," *NPR*, April 11, 2021, https://www.npr.org/2021/04/11/986203268/lee-horton-reflects-on-coming-home-after-years-in-prison.

16. Phil Moore, "The Corona Virus Experiment," *Think*, March 18, 2020, https://thinktheology.co.uk/blog/article/the_corona_virus_experiment.

CHAPTER 3: THE FULLNESS OF CHRIST

1. Warren Wiersbe, *Be Complete* (Wheaton, IL: Victor Books, 1981), 52-53.

2. Lloyd John Ogilvie, *Loved and Forgiven—A Bible Commentary for Laymen: Colossians* (Glendale, CA: 1977), 27-28.

3. John Phillips, *Exploring Colossians & Philemon: An Expository Commentary* (Grand Rapids, MI: Kregel Publications, 2002), 48, 49.

4. "Pastor D. James Kennedy Said in a Sermon," *Sermon Central*, June 18, 2007, https://sermoncentral.com.

5. Robert Jastow, *God and the Astronomers* (Canada: George J. McLeod, Limited, 1992), 177.

6. Nicole Aleindor, "Pastor's lost Bible shows up 15 years later, brings man to Jesus," *The Christian Post*, January 18, 2022.

7. S. Missey Mott Heltzel, "The Pre-eminent Christ," *Christianity Today*, October 12, 1959.

8. "Jesus Film shown in Zambian village," *The Pathway*, February 15, 2022, https://mbcpathway.com/2022/02/15/jesus-film-shown-in-zambian-village/.

9. "'Hacksaw Ridge' Star Boldly Preaches The Gospel On Social Media," *FaithPot*, February 1, 2022, https://faithpot.com/nathaniel-buzolic-faith/.

10. John Phillips, *Exploring Colossians & Philemon: An Expository Commentary* (Grand Rapids, MI: Kregal Publications, 2002), 78.

11. Rob J. Hyndman, "What would convince you?" *Rob J. Hyndman*, accessed February 20, 2022, https://robjhyndman-com/unbelievable/ch4/.

12. Heather Davis Nelson, *Unashamed: Healing Our Brokenness and Finding Freedom From Shame* (Wheaton, IL: Crossway, 2016), 147.

13. R. Kent Hughes, *Colossians and Philemon: The Supremacy of Christ* (Wheaton, IL: Crossway Books, 1989), 40,

14. Kelly Crow, "Botticelli portrait of Jesus Christ sells for $45.4 million," *Fox Business*, January 28, 2022.

CHAPTER 4: AUTHENTIC CHRISTIAN MINISTRY

1. Kaushik Patowary, "The Lighthouse That Wrecked More Ships Than it Saved," *Amusing Planet*, October 17, 2018, https://www.amusingplanet.com/2018/10/the-lighthouse-that-wrecked-more-ships.html and Brad Smithfield, "Built in the wrong place, this Australian lighthouse caused more than 20 shipwrecks," *The Vintage News*, March 7, 2018, https://www.thevintagenews.com/2018/03/07/australian-lighthouse/.

2. John Phillips, *Exploring Colossians & Philemon: An Expository Commentary* (Grand Rapids, MI: Kregel Publications, 2002), 88.

3. R. Kent Hughes, *Colossians and Philemon: The Supremacy of Christ* (Wheaton, IL: Crossway Books, 1989), 247.

4. John Piper, *Filling Up the Afflictions of Christ* (Wheaton, IL: Crossway Books, 2009), 22, 24.

5. R. Kent Hughes, *Colossians and Philemon: The Supremacy of Christ* (Wheaton, IL: Crossway Books, 1989), 47.

6. Timothy Cockes, "Romanian Man Visits American Pastor Who Led Him to Faith 30 Years Earlier," *Church Leaders*, January 14, 2022, https://churchleaders.com/news/414861-romanian-man-visits-american-pastor.html.

7. Warren Wiersbe, *Be Complete* (Colorado Springs, CO: David C. Cook, 2008), 78-79.

8. W. H. Griffith Thomas, *Studies in Colossians and Philemon* (Grand Rapids, MI: Baker Book House, 1973), 70.

9. R. Kent Hughes, *Colossians and Philemon: The Supremacy of Christ* (Wheaton, IL: Crossway Books, 1989), 49.

10. Douglas J. Moo, *The Letters to the Colossians and to Philemon* (Grand Rapids, MI: William B. Eerdmans Publishing Company, 2008), 165.

11. William Barclay, *The Letters to the Philippians, Colossians, and Thessalonians* (Louisville, KY: Westminster John Knox Press, 2003), 150.

12. "Elderly Couple Living in UK's Darkest Village Lights Up the Sky With Huge Christmas Tree They Planted in 1978," *Good News Network*, December 12, 2021, https://www.goodnewsnetwork.org/couple-living-in-darkest-village-lights-sky-with-huge-christmas-tree/.

13. John Phillips, *Exploring Colossians & Philemon: An Expository Commentary* (Grand Rapids, MI: Kregel Publications, 2002), 99.

14. Steven J. Lawson, *Absolutely Sure* (Colorado Springs, CO: Multnomah Books, 1999), 22.

15. Tony Cummings, "Sean Michel: Traveling a road from American Idol to the Delta blues," *Cross Rhythms*, November 30, 2011, https://www.crossrhythms.co.uk/articles/music/Sean_Michel_Travelling_a_road_from_American_Idol_to_the_Delta_blues/45824/p1/.

16. N. T. Wright, *Colossians and Philemon* (Downers Grove, IL: InterVarsity Press, 1986), 99.

17. John Pollock, *The Billy Graham Story* (Grand Rapids, MI: Zondervan, 2003), 43.

18. Warren Wiersbe, *Be Complete* (Colorado Springs, CO: David C. Cook, 2008), 87.

CHAPTER 5: BEWARE

1. Barbara Kantrowitz, "In Search of the Sacred," *Newsweek*, November 28, 1994, 53.

2. Lloyd John Ogilvie, *Loved and Forgiven: A Bible Commentary for Laymen/ Colossians* (Glendale, CA: Regal Books, 1986), 72-73.

3. Adapted from Donald Grey Barnhouse, *Let Me Illustrate* (Grand Rapids, MI: Fleming H. Revell Co., 1994), 230.

4. Ron Dreher, *Live Not By Lies* (New York: Sentinel, 2020), x.

5. Adapted from John Phillips, *Exploring Colossians & Philemon: An Expository Commentary* (Grands Rapids, MI: Kregel Publications, 2002), 114.

6. Christopher Spata, "Tampa Bay woman found love online. The scam cost them 'everything,'" *Tampa Bay Times*, February 9, 2022, https://www.tampabay.com/news/crime/2022/02/09/tampa-bay-women-found-love-online-the-scam-cost-them-everything/.

7. John Phillips, *Exploring Colossians & Philemon: An Expository Commentary* (Grand Rapids, MI: Kregel Publications, 2002), 118.

8. R. Kent Hughes, *Colossians and Philemon: The Supremacy of Christ* (Westchester, IL: Crossway Books, 1989), 78-79.

9. Max Anders, *Holman New Testament Commentary: Galatians, Ephesians, Philippians, and Colossians* (Nashville, TN: Broadman & Holman Publishers, 1999), Kindle Edition.

10. Max Anders, *Holman New Testament Commentary: Galatians, Ephesians, Philippians, and Colossians* (Nashville, TN: Broadman & Holman Publishers, 1999), Kindle Edition.

11. Vance Havner, *Day By Day* (Old Tappan, NJ: Revell, 1953), 6.

12. Max Anders, *Holman New Testament Commentary: Galatians, Ephesians, Philippians, and Colossians* (Nashville, TN: Broadman & Holman Publishers, 1999), Kindle Edition.

13. Quoted by Dennis J. DeHaan, "It Comes with the Ticket," accessed October 18, 2021, https://www.preceptaustin.org/colossians_illustrations_2.

14. "'I Just Knew He Wasn't Going to Scam Me': Long Island Grandmother Helps Catch Alleged Scammer," *CBS News New York*, January 21, 2022, https://newyork.cbslocal.com/2022/01/21/seaford-long-island-grandmother-elderly-scam-suspect-caught/.

CHAPTER 6: WHAT IT MEANS TO BE "IN CHRIST"

1. "Distracted Pedestrians Stumble into Danger," *Akron Beacon Journal*, July 31, 2012, https://www.beaconjournal.com/story/news/nation-world/2012/07/31/distracted-pedestrians-stumble-into-danger/10668275007/.

2. Bob Laurent, *Watchman Nee: Man of Suffering* (Uhrichsville, OH: Barbour Publishing, Inc, u.d.), 67-68.

3. Charles Spurgeon, "Death and Its Sentence Abolished," *The Spurgeon Center*, October 4, 1883, https://www.spurgeon.org/resource-library/sermons/death-and-its-sentence-abolished/#flipbook/.

4. Charles Swindoll, *The Tale of the Tardy Oxcart* (Nashville, TN: Word, 1998), 77.

5. Sharon Dutra, "God Restores What Has Been Taken," *Victorious Living*, accessed February 20, 2022, https://victoriouslivingmagazine.com/2022/01/god-restores-what-has-been-taken/.

6. "Colossians 3:3," *Barnes' Notes on the Bible*, accessed March 15, 2022, https://biblehub.com/commentaries/colossians/3-3.htm.

7. "Secret Hiding Places You've Never Thought Of," *Family Handyman*, August 25, 2021, https://www.familyhandyman.com/list/20-secret-hiding-places/.

8. Lindsay Key, "Training the 21st-Century Country Doctor," *Duke University School of Medicine*, Novermber 16, 2021,https://medschool.duke.edu/stories/training-21st-century-country-doctor.

9. History.com Editors, "Barbara Jo Rubin becomes first female jockey to win race at U.S. thoroughbred track," *History*, February 17, 2022, https://www.history.com/this-day-in-history/notable-female-jockeys-barbara-jo-rubin.

10. John Phillips, *Exploring Colossians & Philemon: An Expository Commentary* (Grand Rapids, MI: Kregel Publications, 2002), 163.

11. Vance Havner, *The Vance Havner Quotebook*, Denis J. Hester, comp. (Grand Rapids, MI: Baker Book House, 1986), 29.

12. Warren Wiersbe, *Be Complete* (Colorado Springs, CO: David C. Cook, 2008), Kindle Edition.

13. Warren Wiersbe, *Be Complete* (Colorado Springs, CO: David C. Cook, 2008), Kindle Edition.

14. John Phillips, *Exploring Colossians & Philemon: An Expository Commentary* (Grand Rapids, MI: Kregel Publications, 2002), 174.

15. WION Web Team, "'Tom Cruise would get angry in a snap of your fingers' reveals actor's ex-manager," *WION*, February 22, 2022, https://www.wionews.com/entertainment/hollywood/news-tom-cruise-would-get-angry-in-a-snap-of-your-fingers-reveals-actors-ex-manager-455212.

16. W. A. Criswell, *Expository Sermons on the Epistle of James* (Grand Rapid, MI: Zondervan, 1975), 63.

17. Curtis Vaughan, *James: A Study Guide* (Grand Rapids, MI: Zondervan, 1969), 69.

18. Max Anders, *Holman New Testament* Commentary: Galatians, Ephesians, Philippians, and Colossians (Nashville, TN: Broadman & Holman Publishers, 1999), Kindle Edition.

19. Randy Alcorn, *The Grace and Truth Paradox* (Colorado Springs, CO: Multnomah Books, 2003), 14.

20. Cody Thomason, "Football Legends Billy Shaw, Richard Price maintain a lifelong friendship," *The Vicksburg Post*, January 27, 2018, https://www.vicksburgpost.com/2018/01/27/football-legends-billy-shaw-richard-price-maintain-a-lifelong-friendship/.

CHAPTER 7: THE CHRISTIAN'S DRESS CODE

1. Ira Shukla, "Forget MET, Here Are 8 Of The Most Expensive Dresses Worn By Celebrities In All Of History," *Scoop Whoop*, September 16, 2021, https://www.scoopwhoop.com/entertainment/most-expensive-dresses-worn-by-celebrities-in-history/.

2. Introduction adapted from Cade Campbell, "Clothed and Unashamed: A Theology of Clothing," *The King's Table*, November 13, 2015, https://kings-table.com/2015/11/13/clothed-and-unashamed-a-theology-of-clothing/.

3. Gerald Ortiz, "Trend Alert: Sunglasses Are All About Candy-Colored Lenses," *GQ*, August 9, 2021, https://www.gq.com/story/best-colored-lens-sunglasses.

4. William Barclay, *The Letters to the Philippians, Colossians, and Thessalonians* (Louisville, KY: Westminster John Knox Press, 2003), Kindle Edition.

5. Alvin J. Schmidt, *How Christianity Changed the World* (Grand Rapids, MI: Zondervan, 2004), 52-53.

6. "11-year-old Orion Jean recognized as Kid of the Year for his commitment to kindness," *ABC Action News 6*, February 21, 2022, https://6abc.com/orion-jean-kid-of-the-year-race-to-kindness-time/11585491/.

7. "TIME 2021 Kid of the Year Orion Jean Lives by Kindness as a Simple Rule, *Parents*, February 17, 2022, https://www.parents.com/kindred/time-for-kids-kid-of-the-year-is-11-year-old-orion-jean/.

8. Pat Williams, *Humility* (Uhrichsville, Ohio: Barbour Publishing, 2016), 230-231.

9. See https://www.gentlebarn.org/.

10. Simeon P. Meads, *Some Suggestions from the Greek of the New Testament* (Berkeley Daily Gazette, 1939), 31.

11. John Wooden, *The Essential Wooden* (New York: McGraw-Hill, 2007), 11.

12. David Mathis, "No Meekness Without Might: What We Learn from Christ's Gentleness," *The Gospel Coalition*, December 24, 2020, https://www.thegospelcoalition.org/article/christ-gentleness/.

13. Adrian Rogers, "Meekness: Do You Have This Quality," September 1, 2020, https://lwf-upgrade.lwf.org/bible-study/meekness-do-you-have-this-quality-1446-bible-study.

14. Warren Wiersbe, *Be Complete* (Colorado Springs, CO: David C. Cook, 2008), Kindle Edition.

15. R. Kent Hughes, *Colossians and Philemon: The Supremacy of Christ* (Wheaton, IL: Crossway Books, 1989), 105.

16. John Phillips, *Exploring Colossians & Philemon: An Expository Commentary* (Grand Rapids, MI: Kregel Publications, 2002), 180.

17. H. W. Craig, *The Sole Sufficiency of Jesus Christ* (London: Marshall, Morgan & Scott, 1961), 82.

18. William Barclay, *The Letters to the Philippians, Colossians, and Thessalonians* (Louisville, KY: Westminster John Knox Press, 2003), Kindle Edition.

19. June DePriest, *A Resting Peace* (Self-published memoir, 2021), 18-21.

20. Tom Olson, "Why do Christians sing?" *Evangelical Magazine*, July/August 2017, https://www.evangelicalmagazine.com/article/why-do-christians-sing/.

21. Jordan Mendoza, "North Carolina sheriff refuses to take down Bible verse in office, says he is 'afraid of burning in hell,'" *USA Today*, December 22, 2021, https://www.usatoday.com/story/news/nation/2021/12/22/bible-verse-nc-sheriff-christianity/8999133002/.

22. Laura Duvall, "In His Name," *Christianity Today*, accessed October 29, 2021, https://www.preachingtoday.com/illustrations/1997/november/3462.html.

23. Warren Wiersbe, *Be Complete* (Colorado Springs, CO: David C. Cook, 2008), Kindle Edition.

24. Story adapted from Michael Green, "Our King's Righteous Attire," accessed October 28, 2021, https://sermons.com/search/results?term=EMPTINESS&category=sermon&sermon_filters=Illustrations&page=7&tab=Illustrations.

CHAPTER 8: THE CHRISTIAN HOUSEHOLD

1. Joseph Chamie, "The end of marriage in America?" *The Hill*, August 10, 2021, https://thehill.com/opinion/finance/567107-the-end-of-marriage-in-america.

2. Michael J. Kruger, "Men, Are You Submissive?" *The Gospel Coalition*, September 30, 2021, https://www.thegospelcoalition.org/article/men-are-you-submissive/.

3. Lori Alexander, "Submission Defined By Elisabeth Elliot," *The Transformed Wife*, June 29, 2018, https://thetransformedwife.com/submission-defined-by-elisabeth-elliott/.

4. Dawn Camp, *The Heart of Marriage* (Grand Rapids, MI: Revell, 2017), foreword.

5. Douglas J. Moo, *The Letters to the Colossians and to Philemon* (Grand Rapids, MI: William B. Eerdmans Publishing Company, 2008), 303.

6. Carmen Kohlruss, "'Their bond was unshakeable,' Fresno County couple died days apart after 37 years together," *The Fresno Bee*, February 14, 2022, https://www.fresnobee.com/news/local/article258315473.html.

7. Jack Canfield, Mark Victor Hansen, and Amy Newmark, *Chicken Soup for the Soul: Married Life!* (Chicken Soup for the Soul Publishing, LLC., 2012), adapted from chapter 1.

8. Alexia Fernandez, "8-Year-Old Ohio Boy Drives His Little Sister to McDonald's After Learning How by Watching YouTube Videos," *People*, April 12, 2017, https://sports.yahoo.com/news/8-old-ohio-boy-drives-232419807.html.

9. Nicole Pelletiere, "Dad Writes 270 Lunchbox Notes to Daughter for Each Day He's Deployed," *ABC News*, November 17, 2020, https://abcnews.go.com/GMA/Family/dad-writes-270-lunchbox-notes-daughter-day-hes/story?id=74166938.

10. Larry Peabody, *Serving Christ in the Workplace* (Fort Washington, PA: CLC Publications, 2013), chapter 1.

11. Cora Hall, "40 Under 40: Jacob L. Ogle leads in real estate development and community," *Knox News*, January 12, 2022, https://www.knoxnews.com/story/money/2022/01/12/knoxville-40-under-40-jake-ogle-scrambled-jakes-five-oaks/8558931002/.

12. Douglas J. Moo, *The Letters to the Colossians and to Philemon* (Grand Rapids, MI: William B. Eerdmans Publishing Company, 2008), 308-309.

13. Quoted in Elisabeth Elliot, *Through Gates of Splendor* (Carol Sream, IL: Tyndale House Publishers, 1986), 20.

14. Dr. Steven R. Cook, "Being the Good Boss," *Linkedin*, October 31, 2019, https://www.linkedin.com/pulse/being-good-boss-dr-steven-r-cook.

CHAPTER 9: CHRISTIAN COMMUNICATION

1. Guy Kawasaki, *Enchantment* (U.S.A.: Penguin, 2011), Kindle Edition.

2. Sam Chan, "Evangelism Isn't a Chore. It's a Joy," *Christianity Today*, March 27, 2020, https://www.christianitytoday.com/ct/2020/ march-web-only/evangelism-is-joy-sam-chan-lent-easter.html.

3. John Stonestreet, "How Prayer Bridged a Generation Gap in My Life," *Christian Headlines*, March 1, 2022, https://www.christianheadlines. com/columnists/breakpoint/how-prayer-bridged-a-generation-gap-in-my-life-and-still-can.html.

4. David A. Morel, *Secret to an Open Door* (Self-published by David A. Morel, 2002), 21-25.

5. Daniel P. Kinkade, "From a Purple Heart to a New Heart," *The Gideons International*, August 13, 2021, https://gideonsinternational.org. uk/2021/08/13/1784/.

6. Benjamin Morrison, "Bomb Shelter Ministry in My Ukrainian Town," *Christianity Today*, March 3, 2022, https://www.christianitytoday.com/ ct/2022/march-web-only/ukraine-russia-bomb-shelter-ministry.html.

7. Homer A. Kent, Jr., *Studies in Colossians and Philemon* (Winona Lake, IN: Baker Book House Company, 1978), 154.

8. "Chinese Church Growth Based On Prayer," *University Heights United Methodist Church*, May 24, 2018, https://www.uhumc.com/post/ chinese-church-growth-based-on-prayer.

9. Daryl Dash, "Vision: Mission (Colossians 4:2-6)," *Dashhouse*, September 27, 2015, https://dashhouse.com/2015927vision-mission-colossians-42-6/.

10. Warren Wiersbe, *Be Complete* (Colorado Springs, CO: David C. Cook, 1981), Kindle Edition.

11. Richard C. Halverson in "No Greater Power," *Christian Reader*, Vol. 25, no. 1.

12. Quoted by Lee and Leslie Strobel in *Spiritual Mismatch* (Grand Rapids, MI: Zondervan, 2017).

13. Max Anders, *Holman New Testament Commentary: Galatians, Ephesians, Philippians, and Colossians* (Nashville, TN: Broadman & Holman Publishers, 1999), Kindle Edition.

14. Shawn A. Akers, "5 Stories of Salvation to Evangelism," *Charisma Leader*, March 10, 2014, https://ministrytodaymag.com/outreach/ evangelism/20728-someone-told-me-evangelism.

15. Max Lucado, "The Power to Change Someone's Life," *Words of Hope and Help*, accessed November 11, 2021, https://maxlucado.com/listen/ power-change-someones-life/.

16. Sinclair Ferguson, *The Power of Words and the Wonder of God* (Wheaton, IL: Crossway, 2009), 66.

17. Russell E. Gehrlein, "My Testimony—How I Came to Faith in Jesus," *Reflections on Theological Topics of Interest*, December 6, 2020, https://regehrlein.wordpress.com/2020/12/06/my-testimony-how-i-came-to-faith-in-jesus/.

CHAPTER 10: PAUL AND HIS FRIENDS

1. Sydney Page, "At age 9, best friends separated fleeing the Nazis. Now, 82 years later, they finally hugged again," *The Washington Post*, November 24, 2021, https://www.washingtonpost.com/lifestyle/2021/11/24/holocaust-reunion-best-friends-shoah/.

2. Adapted from Warren Wiersbe, *Be Complete* (Colorado Springs, CO: David C. Cook, 1981), Kindle Edition.

3. Keith W. Jennison, *The Humorous Mr. Lincoln* (New York: Bonanza Books, 1965), 125-126.

4. Dale Carnegie, *How to Win Friends and Influence People* (New York: Simon and Schuster, 1936), 58.

5. Jack Canfield, Mark Victor Hansen, and Amy Newmark, *Chicken Soup for the Soul: Just Us Girls* (Chicken Soup for the Soul Publishing, 2013), 16-17.

6. William Barclay, *The Letters to the Philippians, Colossians, and Thessalonians* (Louisville, KY: Westminster John Knox Press, 2003), Kindle Edition.

7. William Barclay, *The Letters to the Philippians, Colossians, and Thessalonians* (Louisville, KY: Westminster John Knox Press, 2003), Kindle Edition.

8. Charles Livingstone Allen, *Perfect Peace* (Grand Rapids, MI: F. H. Revell Company, 1979), 139.

9. Tim Smith, "6 Minutes: There's Nothing Tougher," *Hometown Life*, February 25, 2017, https://hometownlife.com/story/sports/high-school/2017/02/25/6-minutes-theres-nothing-tougher-prep-wrestling-high-school-michigan-state-finals/98064896/.

10. Brian Blackwell, "A mighty movement of God: First Lafayette prayed for revival, 56 baptized!" *Baptist Message*, February 28, 2022, https://www.baptistmessage.com/a-mighty-movement-of-god-first-lafayette-prayed-for-revival-56-baptized/.

11. Quoted by Emma Pattee, "How to Have Closer Friendships (and Why You Need Them)," *The New York Times*, November 20, 2019, https://www.nytimes.com/2019/11/20/smarter-living/how-to-have-closer-friendships.html.

12. "22 Heartwarming Stories of True Friendship That Will Make You Call Your Bestie," *Reader's Digest*, July 20, 2021, https://www.rd.com/article/stories-of-friendship/.

13. Warren Wiersbe, *Be Complete* (Colorado Springs, CO: David C. Cook, 1981), 172.

14. John Dunlop, MD, *Finishing Well to the Glory of God* (Wheaton, IL: Crossway, 2011), 21-22.

15. William Barclay, *The Letters to the Philippians, Colossians, and Thessalonians* (Louisville, KY: Westminster John Knox Press, 2003), Kindle Edition.

ADDITIONAL RESOURCES

FROM DAVID JEREMIAH

Count It All Joy

When the apostle Paul wrote to the church at Philippi, his letter had one recurring theme: Joy in the Lord. Paul spent two years under arrest in Rome, chained to a Roman guard—no doubt it was not a happy time, and yet he was full of joy.

In *Count It All Joy*, Pastor David Jeremiah takes us on a journey through the book of Philippians, where Paul mentions joy sixteen times in four short chapters. This verse-by-verse study of Paul's powerful letter offers insights on how the joy of the Lord provides strength and encouragement to the believer in every situation we face in life.

What to Do When You Don't Know What to Do

How many self-help books are on your bookshelf at home? As helpful as those resources may be, they do not offer counsel for the real problems that occur in everyday life—but the book of James does—it offers the wisdom we need to live for the glory of God.

In *What to Do When You Don't Know What to Do*, Dr. Jeremiah examines the book of James verse-by-verse and line-by-line. Through this study, you will gain practical and life-changing knowledge on how to react as a believer in every kind of circumstance. And by embracing the truths found there, the peace that comes from following Christ and obeying God's Word will be yours.

FURTHER YOUR STUDY OF GOD'S WORD

· · · · · · · ·

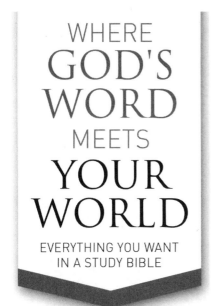

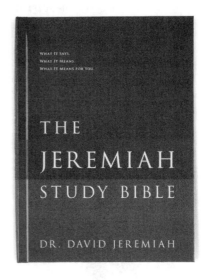

MORE THAN 500,000 PEOPLE
ARE USING **THE JEREMIAH STUDY BIBLE**

The Jeremiah Study Bible is comprehensive, yet easy to understand. More than forty years in the making, it is deeply personal and designed to transform your life. No matter your place or time in history, Scripture always speaks to the important issues of life. Hear God speak to you through studying His Word in *The Jeremiah Study Bible*.

NOW AVAILABLE IN:

• New Kings James Version • Large Print NKJV
• New International Version • English Standard Version

Request your Study Bible today:
www.DavidJeremiah.org/JSB

STAY CONNECTED

Take advantage of two great ways to let David Jeremiah
give you spiritual direction every day!

Both are absolutely free!

Turning Points Magazine and Devotional

Receive David Jeremiah's magazine, *Turning Points*, each month. Each
magazine features:

- A monthly study focus
- Relevant articles
- Special features

- Daily devotional readings
- Bible study resource offers
- Live event schedule

Request *Turning Points* magazine today!

Click: www.DavidJeremiah.org/Magazine
Call: (800) 947-1993

Your Daily Turning Point E-Devotional

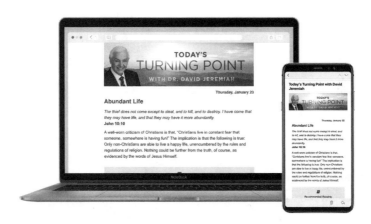

Start your day off right! Find words of inspiration and spiritual motivation waiting for you on your computer every morning! You can receive a daily e-devotional from David Jeremiah that will strengthen your walk with God and encourage you to live the authentic Christian life.

Request your free e-devotional today!

Click: www.DavidJeremiah.org/Devo

Call: (800) 947-1993

Books Written by David Jeremiah

Escape the Coming Night

Count It All Joy

The Handwriting on the Wall

Invasion of Other Gods

Angels—Who They Are and How They Help ... What the Bible Reveals

The Joy of Encouragement

Prayer—The Great Adventure

God in You

Stories of Hope

Slaying the Giants in Your Life

My Heart's Desire

Sanctuary

The Things That Matter

The Prayer Matrix

31 Days to Happiness—Searching for Heaven on Earth

When Your World Falls Apart

Turning Points

Discover Paradise

Captured by Grace

Grace Givers

Why the Nativity?

Signs of Life

Life-Changing Moments with God

Hopeful Parenting

1 Minute a Day—Instant Inspiration for the Busy Life

Grandparenting—Faith That Survives Generations

In the Words of David Jeremiah

What in the World Is Going On?

The Sovereign and the Suffering

The 12 Ways of Christmas

What to Do When You Don't Know What to Do

Living with Confidence in a Chaotic World

The Prophecy Answer Book

The Coming Economic Armageddon

Pathways, Your Daily Walk with God

What the Bible Says About Love, Marriage, and Sex

I Never Thought I'd See the Day

Journey, Your Daily Adventure with God

The Unchanging Word of God

God Loves You: He Always Has—He Always Will

Discovery, Experiencing God's Word Day by Day

Destination, Your Journey with God

Answers to Questions About Heaven

Answers to Questions About Spiritual Warfare

Answers to Questions About Adversity

Quest—Seeking God Daily

The Upward Call

Ten Questions Christians Are Asking

Understanding the 66 Books of the Bible

A.D.—The Revolution That Changed the World

Agents of the Apocalypse

Agents of Babylon

Reset—Ten Steps to Spiritual Renewal

People Are Asking ... Is This the End?

30 Days of Prayer

Hope for Today

Hope—An Anchor for Life

Mission Quest

Revealing the Mysteries of Heaven

Answers to Questions About Prophecy

A Life Beyond Amazing: 9 Decisions That Will Transform Your Life Today

Greater Purpose

Discovery: Understanding the 66 Books of the Bible for Kids

The God You May Not Know

Overcomer: 8 Ways to Live a Life of Unstoppable Strength, Unmovable Faith, and Unbelievable Power

In Moments Like These

The Book of Signs

Everything You Need: 8 Essential Steps to a Life of Confidence in the Promises of God

Daily in His Presence

Answers to Questions About Living in the Last Days

The Jesus You May Not Know

Shelter in God

Forward: Discovering God's Presence and Purpose in Your Tomorrow

Strength for Today

Hope—Living Fearlessly in a Scary World

Answers to Questions About the Bible

God Has Not Forgotten You

Where Do We Go From Here?: How Tomorrow's Prophecies Foreshadow Today's Problems

Every Day With Jesus

After the Rapture

Living the 66 Books of the Bible

Answers to Questions About Prayer